The Prevalence of Deceit

Also by F. G. Bailey

Caste and the Economic Frontier, 1957
Tribe, Caste, and Nation, 1960
Politics and Social Change, 1963
Stratagems and Spoils, 1969
Gifts and Poison (ed.), 1971
Debate and Compromise (ed.), 1973
Morality and Expediency, 1977
The Tactical Uses of Passion, 1983
Humbuggery and Manipulation, 1988

The Prevalence of Deceit

F. G. Bailey

Cornell University Press

Ithaca and London

First published 1991 by Cornell University Press.

International Standard Book Number 0-8014-2542-5 (cloth)
International Standard Book Number 0-8014-9773-6 (paper)
Library of Congress Catalog Card Number 90-42148

Printed in the United States of America

Librarians: Library of Congress cataloging information appears on the last page of the book.

♾ The paper in this book meets the minimum requirements of the American National Standard for Information Sciences—Permanence of Paper for Printed Library Materials, ANSI Z39.48-1984.

Contents

Contents

Acknowledgments

For prompt and pertinent comments I thank my colleagues Roy D'Andrade, Paula Levin, Tanya Luhrmann, Jim Moore, and Fitz Poole.

F. G. B.

Preface

And even the most fanatical ideology must adjust itself to revealed truth or perish. The job is to cling everlastingly to the truth: to try everlastingly to find it in the clatter and confusion of these times—and to find it even in the storm of words of a political campaign.

That was Adlai Stevenson, campaigning in the autumn of 1954, the same Adlai Stevenson who, seven years later, failed to cling hard enough to the truth when he talked to the United Nations about what his country was doing in the Bay of Pigs.[1] Whether he lied or was misinformed is not clear; certainly now his name is associated, to a degree unusual for a politician, with honesty and integrity. He was also, of course, the candidate who twice tried and twice failed to win the presidency, and his career might suggest that failure goes along with resolute honesty or, perhaps, with reluctant and halfhearted dishonesty.[2]

Sometimes there is indeed "clatter and confusion." When the Prison Officers' Association in California gave assembly member Sonny Mojonnier ten thousand dollars in recognition of action "beyond the call of duty" (she rose from a sick bed to vote in their interest), they proclaimed they were giving an award for public

[1]The reference is to President Kennedy's failed attempt in 1961 to terminate Castro's rule in Cuba by sponsoring an invading force of Cuban exiles.

[2]The quotation comes from the *Los Angeles Times Magazine*, July 17, 1988. The United Nations incident is briefly reported in Wise 1973:52–54.

service. When the predictable storm broke, she pointed out that she had already voted when the award was made, did not know about it beforehand, and therefore could not have been influenced by the payment. The payment, she insisted, was merely a speaker's fee for a brief talk given when accepting the award.[3] *Award* versus *bribe* versus *fee* then becomes an issue among Mojonnier, her supporters, and her detractors, each asserting their own truth, each placing the payment in a different context and so giving it a different meaning.

Attitudes toward truth and standards of truth telling vary. Years ago I was treated to a lecture on the comparative sociology of dishonesty from a minister in the Orissa government.[4] He was deploring the current level of moral turpitude in Orissa and comparing it with that in Britain (which he had never visited). He told me that milk in Britain was delivered in bottles to the doorstep and even if you and your cook stayed in bed half the morning, no one stole the milk. Even more incredible was the report of a current scandal in Britain, where a minister of the crown was on trial for corruption: when confronted with the bribe, a bottle of whisky, "He fainted clean away! Imagine it! A mere bottle of whisky and he faints clean away! And it's cheaper there, too!"

Not everyone has Adlai Stevenson's positive concern for truth. The Saami—more generally known as Lapps—go one long step beyond even Machiavelli and make a game of untruth.

Lying, bluff, secrecy, and espionage are all coordinated into their dealing with non-Saami and nonhumans and in their daily routines with other Saami, to form an instrumental and expressive drama. The challenge for Saami actors resides in orchestrating a distinctive social character in which one's reputation as a humorous, clever and sporty deceiver exceeds that as an excessive, trivial and malicious one. Moreover, individuals expect others,

---

[3]In that case she owed them another four speeches, since a "political" honorarium in California at that time was limited to two thousand dollars for each appearance.

[4]Orissa is a state in the Federal Republic of India.

including herding dogs, reindeer, and ethnographers, to behave deceptively. (Anderson 1986:342–43)

My academic colleagues who have risen above scholarship and teaching to become administrators or dedicated committee members could benefit from this example of Saami, who are at least straightforward about their own lack of virtue. The academic arena, too, is populated by deceivers, whether sporty or malicious or obsessed with triviality, public-spirited gamesters enjoying their politics. But very few would concede that mostly it is a game (the spoils being often of little substantive value); still less would they admit to enjoyment.[5] But most of them do little harm. Moreover, if my argument is correct, since they are contenders for power, they could not do otherwise than practice deceit while being enthusiasts for truth.

I have always—like most people—been entertained or puzzled (and occasionally distressed) by the various forms of dishonesty or guile or make-believe without which we do not seem to be able to manage our social and political life. But for a long time it did not occur to me that it was within my anthropologist's competence to investigate them.

There was a reason; my intellectual lenses had been designed to filter out things like guile. I was then—about thirty years ago—a simple positivist, in touch with truth and therefore happy. Whether or not it was Adlai Stevenson's "revealed" truth, I am not sure, because he doesn't say from where the revelation comes; but truth was clear enough to me, proved and empirically demonstrated, positive truth, the fruit of rationality and observation—in a word, *scientific*. I did not quite sink to the level of saying that the facts spoke for themselves, being aware that facts (or data—at that time facts and data seemed much the same thing) are theory generated. But I eschewed metaphysical spec-

[5]The sporting aspects of academic politics are considered at length in Bailey 1977.

ulation and tried to write only what was buttressed by evidence. I knew that outside ourselves was a natural world, regular, objective, comprehensible if we studied it the right way. Consequently I was uncomfortable talking about minds, because that led to a problem then called "psychological reality," or "How do you know what is really in anyone's mind, even your own?" I liked to work in what I took to be the "real" world of facts, of historical events, a world of action, for the most part unambiguous, explicit, and intelligible.

I also knew there were certain axiomatic truths (by no means all of them located in the positivist scriptures), so obvious that they hardly needed enunciation. For example, you could take it for granted (like Edmund Leach) that motivations usually had to do with power and advantage; that making a living called the tune for other activities (Peter Worsley); that in the end all problems could be made to yield to reason because that is how scientists solve problems and we were, after all, engaged in building a natural science of society (A. R. Radcliffe-Brown); that culture was a mere epiphenomenon, secondary to the basic social structure (any structural-functionalist); that every man had his price (the economist W. Arthur Lewis); that God usually was on the side of the big battalions (Voltaire, who later changed his mind and said He favored not the big battalions but the best shots); and so forth.[6]

Of course, the question of motivations, and of the part played by emotions, was troublesome; but if one kept the vision distant enough, one could, for example, point out that a redistribution of wealth led to a redistribution of power, without ever exploring what was in the minds of those who were losing or gaining power. But the redistribution of which I am thinking—between

[6]Leach 1954; Worsley 1956; Radcliffe-Brown 1957. W. Arthur Lewis, an otherwise sensitive and intelligent economist, wrote: "Many countries have indeed attitudes and institutions which inhibit growth, but they will rid themselves of these attitudes and institutions as soon as their people discover that they stand in the way of economic opportunities" (Foreword to Epstein 1962:ix).

castes in Bisipara[7]—led to a lot of altercation and displays of loud passion and a little violence, and one had to wonder why people behaved that way instead of following the dictates of reason and recognizing reality for what it was (what *I* saw it to be). That in turn led to speculation about what must have been in their minds (and why their minds failed to match mine) to make them show such passion and behave so unreasonably. Moreover, although the distant vision (that economic changes had altered the balance of power within the village) was clearly correct and could be proved empirically by demonstrating that those who lost control of land also lost power, it seemed to leave out of account much that was interesting: not just the sound and fury of passions but also (and more worrying because it concerned rationality) the cognitive side of the matter—the schemes and stratagems that the various contestants employed to resist the process of change or to push it along faster.

So I found myself writing about their ideas and feelings as if they were causes of action. But when I did so, I reassured myself that this was not really a betrayal of honest positivism; it was merely a convenient way to describe what was going on. A refusal ever to reify (never talking about ideas or culture "doing" things) costs out very heavily in long-windedness. It made sense to keep things short and refer to ambitions, obligations, even scruples and various other intangible human features that could not be observed directly. But I certainly did not intend to imply that sentiments or ideas or culture had any causal significance; they were, I told myself, not *explanations* for the way people behaved; they were just convenient shorthand *descriptions* of that behavior. Nonetheless, I found that most of what I wrote was couched in the framework of "What on earth was in their minds to make them behave that way?"

Now I have seen the light (I think). I have been born again

7The events I am referring to are described in Bailey 1957. Bisipara is a village in the state of Orissa, India.

(somewhat). I still like simplicity, being irritated beyond endurance by some Frenchmen and most postmodernist colleagues who foreground aphorism and paradox and parade a self-indulgent crocodile sensibility for the person they call the Other, thus—the style is infectious—making an occultation for their intellectual confusions and ideational vacuity. More about them in a moment. I think I am still a positivist of sorts (experience can prove some ideas wrong, even if it takes a long time), but I am no longer a simple positivist.[8] I am therefore also less happy, because I know that absolute and objective truth, if it exists at all, is not easily found. Words and symbols are to the front, presenting us with the social construction of an external reality that has retreated into the shadows. I have lived too long with colleagues who write variously about *representations, constructs, understandings*, and even (barbarizing a perfectly good Greek plural) *schemas*, not to mention *needs* and *drives*, and who blithely assume that in those words and their associated conceptual frameworks lies sufficient understanding of why people behave the way they do. So I am somewhat reformed, born again halfway into culture and cognition, perhaps even a step or two in the direction of psychodynamics. I am content now to do my thinking in the framework of "What on earth is in their minds to make them behave that way?"

But even if I do suffer from idealist tendencies, I have no illusions about really getting into other people's minds, and more than a few doubts about getting even into my own. Other people's minds are apt to be impenetrable, and the contents of my own mind are obscured by a combination of the Freudian unconscious and Bourdieu's *habitus* (the taken-for-granted part of culture).[9] So all I can do is watch what people (myself included) do and say, and use whatever interpretive theories seem suitable to infer what must be in their minds. Whether the result is a short-

---

[8]These confessions, of course, are rhetoric, not plain description; they are intended to do what the Cretan did when he proclaimed all Cretans liars.

[9]Bourdieu 1982.

hand description or an explanation does not worry me: it is useful, whatever it is, because it lets one try to predict how they might behave in other contexts.

Of course the prediction is very unsure. Various interpretive theories are available, and it is not always clear how to choose between them. The data themselves are always contestable, being conditioned by the theory used to select them. Furthermore, when people talk and do things, they are usually aware that they are sending out messages from which other people will try to read what is in their minds. But everyone has the power to conceal motives and intentions or even to sow misleading clues. If people want to "bias the situation" (to borrow a neat euphemism from an academic dean who was very skilled at doing so), they modify (that is, falsify) their speech and their actions.

So people tell lies about themselves and their motives and even about their actions. That "fact"—one handles the word gingerly—would have been a considerable embarrassment to me in my salad days of positivism if I had not believed that truth somehow emerged in action, which, of course, it does not, except in a rather gross sense that I will come to in the concluding chapter. Eventually the guiding light at the end of my tunnel proved to be rhetoric, the notion that words and other performances are messages that can be used to manipulate other people. But I might have been lost entirely, like some of my colleagues gone astray, because there is a side branch to this tunnel that, in my vision at least, has no light at its end. It is the study of rhetoric purely as discourse, as a thing in itself removed entirely from the world of action, permitting no reality except the text itself. I am referring initially to hermeneutics (on weekdays termed interpretivism) and especially to that congeries of jargon-infested writings called postmodernism, which only now is beginning to vacate the anthropological foreground. Its presence is signaled overtly by such key words as *deconstruction*, *intertextuality*, and the ever-present but hapless *Other*, who always seems to be getting suckered. There is also a string of favored code words that serve to identify the true-believer and to exclude those who have not seen the light: discourse, poetics, empowerment, self-reflexivity, foreground and privilege (both as verbs), the joyous and ubiquitous identification of oxymoron, and an irritating habit of startling the reader into wakefulness with unlikely punlike sundering hyphenations (which is an oxymoron, of course), such as pre-text (a scripture falsely claimed to justify authority) or exorbitant (meaning "not in orbit" or "unusual") or id-entity (our nastier part).[10] Nevertheless, pretentious parlor jargon notwithstanding, the movement has its uses, even importance, and one of my goals is to exploit those uses without entirely abandoning positivism: not, certainly, to reconcile the varieties of idealism with any kind of positivism (a mountainous endeavor best left to the latter-day critical theorists, who have breath enough to pontificate at that altitude) but just to get samples of both into the toolkit. When one is selecting ideas, intellectual elegance (the aesthetic side of things) and even logic take second place behind usefulness. That piece of common sense will be aired again, and more fully considered, in the final chapter.

Mostly I am going to write about people in power or people who would like to have power or to avoid having it exercised over them, because, as is well known, there is a close connection between deceit and power.

Sometimes the deceit is quite straightforward. At the present time in the United States it has become almost taken for granted that no politician can survive close scrutiny of his conduct from an ethical point of view. Honest politicians are few and, like Adlai Stevenson or President Carter, not destined for the Politicians' Hall of Fame. The *Los Angeles Times*, on April 14, 1989, reported that ten years earlier the City Club of San Diego had sponsored a lecture series with the title "San Diego Inside: The Power Structure and How It Works." The lectures were given by

[10]These texts, appearing to be reader-unfriendly, because they exact alertness, are in fact aggressively flirtatious, feeling out the reader, as when deadpan Tyler (1987:91) prints "Neur," which is not a misprint but a coy reference to Evans-Pritchard's tasteless pun in the introductory chapter to *The Nuer*.

some of the outstanding citizens of the time, men who had made their mark in public life. A lecture on *politics* was delivered by a gentleman subsequently brought to trial for conspiracy and perjury. Two lectures were about *justice*: one given by a chief of police who was later involved in a scandal over fixing traffic tickets for his friends, the other by a Superior Court judge who afterward got into trouble for drunk driving and for mishandling a five-million-dollar fund entrusted to his care. The lecturer on *money* was the occasion in 1989 for this somewhat snide remembrance of 1978: he had just been arrested on a charge of laundering large sums of what he believed to be Colombian drug money.

This lack of probity is generally considered to be endemic in the political community. If you are looking for the most outstanding deceptions, you will find them in politics (just as the best fantasies are found in religion). "Is it honest?" said a talk-show anchorman, "Or is it just politics?" and he said it innocently, without a smile.[11] But, before concluding that politicians are crooked and the rest of us are not, we should remember that the word *politics* means more than the people who govern countries or cities: power is everywhere—in the family, in the classroom, in university administrations, in hospitals, in sport, in marriage, even in friendships and (sad to say) loving.

But matters are not always so straightforward as in cases of perjury, embezzlement, or laundering drug money. There is a marked ambivalence and considerable confusion about truth itself: we profess to adore it but also sometimes find it threatening. Error, of course, is bad. So is deceit: but not always, and some forms of untruth are admired. There are in fact many forms of untruth, and the very richness of our own language (and, I suppose, other languages too) helps make it difficult in daily life to pin down a plain lie. There is a slippage, hard to control, among deceit and error and fiction.

But that has not stopped people from trying to get a firm grasp on truth. They know *what* it is: truth is everything that is the

[11]*MacNeil/Lehrer NewsHour*, August 21, 1988.

case. But what is easily defined is not so easily identified, and the problem is to know what is in fact the case. Two kinds of answer have been produced. One (somewhat sophisticated) is that truth is a matter of convention, what people agree to be true (truth as coherence, or "intersubjectivity is objectivity," as the jargon goes), and sometimes there is added the slightly nervous stipulation that the people concerned should be qualified, reasonable, and ready to listen to one another's arguments, like dialecticians. Truth is then somewhat optional, unconstrained by nature, a matter of collective choice, man-made: truth is what qualified people collectively decide is truth. Deciding who is qualified is similarly a matter of collective judgment, so there is plenty of room for argument.

The other truth (common sense and my simple positivism) is an imperative, theoretically leaving no room for argument: God's truth, anchored in nature, an objective reality to which all must conform and correspondence with which decides whether a statement is true or false. There are various techniques for getting at this reality, one of them being a combination of experiment and those same dialectical procedures used to arrive at intersubjective truth. Reasonable civilized people put one point of view against another, testing each in turn, until they jointly uncover the truth, which (for those who deny that intersubjectivity makes objectivity) is waiting out there in the world to be uncovered. Unfortunately, when we come to examine a notable example of practical dialecticians in active pursuit of social and political truth (Gandhi's satyagraha), what they do looks less like a search for truth than a contest for power.

Truth and deceit are inextricably entangled with power: accepting that fact opens two further lines of inquiry. One is about collusive lying, which occurs when people collaborate (willingly or otherwise) in pretending that circumstances are other than they know them in fact to be. What they collude in is a "basic lie." This kind of behavior is ubiquitous, and it has important stabilizing functions both for individuals and for their societies. On the other hand, it can also lead to disaster through ignoring the demands of a changing reality. The destabilizing maneuver is simple but not necessarily effective: just brand the basic lie as not the truth at all, saying that in reality it is mere fiction or ordinary falsehood or a hegemonic lie perpetrated by the ruling classes.

The other line of inquiry is about adversarial lying: how to win the power game by not telling the truth or by imposing on others your own version of the basic lie or manipulating them into accepting it. Lies protect the weak from the strong, and the strong bamboozle the weak with myths about *noblesse oblige* and the like, countered by other myths that serve, with varying degrees of double-dealing, as weapons for the weak.

We live our lives pointed psychologically in two opposite directions. On the one hand, we yearn for order and discipline and a world in which truth prevails. In words at least, most of us support the institutions that stand for law and order and good government and "natural justice" and so forth. These institutions are needed, we evidently believe, because there is not enough virtue in people to make them behave with the proper altruism. No one is above the law, not even Oliver North, believing he is obeying the president's command.[12] On the other hand, if Oliver North must stay within the law, how can he show the initiative that is expected from a warrior in a covert war? Even for ordinary people going about their daily business, institutions are restraints; worse, they may be predatory, like the tax collector, demanding more and more and often experienced as oppressive and unfair. Then they drive us into trying to "beat the system," thus demonstrating to others that there really is a shortage of virtue and at the same time convincing ourselves that no one, not even good people like ourselves, can live by virtue alone.

If you turn the coin over, you find people pleading the opposite

[12]Memories are short and Oliver North is already out of the headlines. The reference is to his role in the so-called Iran-Contra scandal, which arose when it was discovered that certain members of President Reagan's administration were engaged in various covert and illegal activities in order to supply money and arms to the "Contras," who were mounting an insurrection against the Marxist government of Nicaragua.

cause, asking for more regulation. First they say that government has no business in the marketplace, and they keep on saying that until, like the Chrysler corporation a few years back or the savings and loan institutions at the present time, they need government to save them from the consequences of their own incompetence. Then there is a demand for more government intervention. From either direction, the attitude is the same. We want both order and freedom and are reluctant to admit that these things are in complementary distribution: where one is found, the other is not.[13]

The discipline of a social framework is exercised through basic lies (which, of course, purport to be objective truth). They are collusive pretenses, whether forced or unforced, that control and restrict and bring order. They fix as "truth" what hitherto was ambiguous and arguable, and in doing so they limit our freedom to act for ourselves, to innovate, to invent, to make fiction and fantasy, to charm, and to deceive—all those unroutinized creative things that save us from being automatons. We can oppose one basic lie with a different one—capitalism with communism or whatever—but that still leaves us with the same problem because it is no more than a change of one straitjacket for another. "Freedom and Whisky gang thegither!" said Robert Burns. Freedom comes only from injecting into the institutional bloodstream its antigens: ambiguity, spontaneity, uncertainty, irresponsibility, and—the subject of this essay—untruth.

The part of us that yearns for order, no less than the part that wants freedom, can hardly find that statement comforting; either way we are faced with untruth. If order itself rests upon a basic lie and freedom also requires untruths, the inescapable conclusion is that no form of social interaction can entirely dispense with untruth. Can that really be so? Does reality set *no* limits on untruths? Are we not constrained by an objective truth, by hard

---

[13]A neat rhetorical device (another oxymoron) is to insist that the truest freedom is experienced only through total surrender of the self to a divinity ("whose service is perfect freedom") or to a collectivity.

reality, by the brute facts of nature? Science, it may be said by those who are not scientists, deals in objective truth. But the scientists themselves do not see their work that way. They see it as dealing not with objective truth but with convenient fictions that are upheld so long as they continue to be useful. It may also be said, by scientists and nonscientists alike, that science, by teaching us how to accommodate ourselves to nature, allows us to control it and in that way brings us freedom, from nature itself and, of course, from the religious dogmas and superstitions that formerly controlled us. But there are others (usually not scientists) who brand the scientific attitude as the ultimate arrogance, a world constructed without morality, the very negation of our humanity and, because imperative, a most effective rhetoric of regimentation.

In the final chapter I will return to these and similar questions. In particular I will ask how well, if at all, the upholders of one orthodoxy can communicate with unbelievers; and I will endeavor to show that the domain of action and its consequences, at least in politics, *ultimately* determines the fate of ideas. But in the meantime—until the consequences are reaped—might is right, and right presents itself as "truth." If that is so, then one must ask whether ethics are an issue at all when a politician (or anyone else) tries to do what Adlai Stevenson so strongly urged: "cling everlastingly to the truth."

So, having opened the closet, let us see what is in there to help us find the truth about how people use "truth" and "deceit." Certainly, if we had surer ways to identify truth, deceit might be less prevalent. Certainly, many people try sincerely to avoid deceit. The *idea* of truth looms large in our lives: it does much for us and we could not survive without it. But at the same time truth itself remains elusive and, I will argue, is mostly illusory. The life that we share with others must include untruth in one or more of its three forms: deceit, error, or fiction. Life—certainly political life—is then a dialogue between those three and the illusion of truth.

Preface

The territory is certainly not unsurveyed, but the maps often do not match. In the first chapter, I examine some philosophical street guides to the city of the eternal verities. None of them exactly fits what the visitor finds; but also none of them is entirely out of touch with reality. Metaphysical and epistemological speculations are put aside in the two chapters that follow, and behavior that links truth with power is examined: first, "truth" in the form of the collusive "basic lie" and, second, the use of lies as weapons. The final chapter argues that the best view of ourselves and our interactions is got when sitting on the fence. We are not constrained to see our world only as our various cultures tell us to see it, which is the position of relativism in its various forms, including the extreme of postmodernism. Sooner or later a real world of experience will intrude, and make us change those parts of our culture which we decide are not doing the job we want them to do. But—and this is how I find myself sitting on the fence—the linkage between experience and ideas is extremely loose because it is continually being tinkered with by those concerned with exercising power or with frustrating other peoples' attempts to dominate or manipulate them.

F. G. BAILEY

Del Mar, California

The Prevalence of Deceit

1 | What Is Truth?

[Jesus said] *To this end was I born, and for this cause came I into the world, that I should bear witness unto the truth. Everyone that is of the truth heareth my voice.*
   Pilate saith unto him. *What is truth?*
   —John 18:37–38

Turning and turning in the widening gyre
The falcon cannot hear the falconer;
Things fall apart; the centre cannot hold;
Mere anarchy is loosed upon the world.
                    —W. B. Yeats, *The Second Coming*

Turning and Turning

   Lies generally get a bad press. When Emilia denounces Iago, the cadences are beautiful but the adjectives seem almost redundant:

> "You told a lie, an odious damned lie;
> Upon my soul, a lie, a wicked lie."

Lies are odious; so much so that the word itself is unclean, an abomination, and we search out euphemisms to keep our mouths clean. Children, in my childhood, did not lie; they told "stories" or "fibs."[1] When they were older and less innocent and went to school, a particularly brazen, barefaced lie was called a "whopper." Still later, well past the age of innocence, sitting on a committee and pondering a report that might be embarrassing if submitted in that form to higher authorities, people might suggest a "constructive revision" of the document. The former head of the Civil Service of the United Kingdom and secretary to the Cabinet Sir Robert Armstrong, cross-examined before an Australian court in the Spycatcher affair,[2] refused to agree that a letter he had written "contained a lie." It did give a "misleading impression," he admitted, but there was no "straight untruth." Counsel asked him if it was perhaps a "bent untruth." Sir Robert then made his mark in history; it was, he said (borrowing from Edmund Burke), no more than "being economical with the truth."[3]

Lies are dangerous because, wrote Francis Bacon, "a lie faces God, and shrinks from man" (1909:9). Therefore we not only shrink from the word but also protect ourselves magically, as children, by crossing our fingers when telling a lie to neutralize God's anger. The adult version is the grotesque "mental reservation" (Bok 1979:37–39), which converts a brazen lie into the literal truth by means of an inaudible addition.

"George, did you cut down my cherry tree?"
"No, father! [*sotto voce*—not with my *big* axe!]."

God, unlike George's father, is tuned in to mental reservations and thus has not been faced with a lie.

Truth, on the other hand, usually gets a good press. For Bacon

[1]The noun, my dictionary says, is derived from "fable." It must also be "fabrication," something manufactured, something not part of the natural order. I will have more to say about the family of untruths—lies, fantasy, myths, public relations handouts, and so forth—later.
[2]This was a stubborn and unsuccessful attempt by Mrs. Thatcher's government to suppress an autobiography by a former member of the British secret services.
[3]I take this exchange from a brief report in the *Guardian*, July 30, 1988.

it is "the sovereign good of human nature" (1909:8). "Divine melodious truth" said Keats. Truth has a "bright countenance" in Milton; and in Jane Austen: "My Emma, does not everything serve to prove more and more the beauty of truth and sincerity in all our dealings with each other?" Moreover, so it is assumed, truth is within the reach of everyone wise enough to employ it. Gandhi was unequivocal: "Truthfulness is the master-key. Do not lie under any circumstances whatsoever, keep nothing secret, take your teachers and your elders into your confidence and make a clean breast of everything to them" (Bondurant 1965:22, quoted from *Young India* December 25, 1925). That sounds straightforward, simple, and very reassuring. Goodness is attainable; and truth is part of goodness. Things will not fall apart. But in fact truth and truthfulness are not so simple.

First—and strangely—truth does not always have a "bright countenance"; the word "truth" can also suggest authority, dominance, an unyielding absolutism. Francis Bacon, using a single telling adjective, filled out Saint John's story of the encounter at the crucifixion: " '*What is truth?*' said jesting Pilate, and would not stay for an answer" (1909:7). Evidently something has made Pilate disdainful. Why the mockery? The answer surely lies in the biblical version and in that definite article: "*the* truth." "*The* truth" implies that there is only *one* truth. It is a phrase with a bullying assertive tone, lacking humility, a posture of undeniable and inescapable superiority, an *I-know-better-than-you* quality. It is, to say the least, irritating. It closes our options, limits our freedom of action. It intimidates; it excludes. *The* truth is the end of asking questions; doubt is not just a mistake; it becomes a sin. That is why "true-believer" has become a phrase of mockery, and we use it to dismiss presumptuous and peremptory authority. Pilate was right to deride a claim to monopolize *the* truth.

On that occasion he was also clever enough to save himself from a sermon by not asking what was the *particular* truth that Jesus witnessed. Instead, a skeptical administrator, he asked that somewhat despairing question: "What is truth?" Thus, politely, he slighted true-believership. If he did not stay for an answer, one can sympathize, because the answers are many and contradictory, as we will see.

Mr. Speakes, a former "spokesman" for the Reagan White House, published a book in 1988 revealing among other things that he had invented quotable quotations and falsely attributed them to the president. Feeling that his man was putting up a poor "media" performance compared with Gorbachev at the conference held in Iceland, the happily named Speakes came up with: "There is much that divides us, but I believe the world breathes easier because we are talking here together," indeed a statesmanlike utterance, but composed by Speakes and never said by Reagan. In the *Los Angeles Times* of April 15, 1988, after Speakes had revealed this mild and surely well-intentioned duplicity, there appeared an essay, which had in it some familiar sentiments: "The point is that, in the end, there is no real moral or political distinction between the small lies and the large, the false quotes and the false policies. All sprang from an abiding mistrust, fear and contempt of the public, a deep-seated refusal and inability to conduct the truly open and honest government on which a democracy depends."

Of course journalists have an ax to grind, wanting to bring everything out in the open, but my guess is that most people who read the *Los Angeles Times* essay took it with a grain of salt and few of them felt a genuine sense of moral outrage. Certainly Mr. Speakes himself did not.

What is strange and even rather eerie about this is Mr Speakes's attitude towards what he did. True, he says that "in retrospect, it was clearly wrong to take such liberties," but he means "wrong" only in the sense of risking having the Russians blow the whistle on him: "Luckily the Russians didn't dispute the quotes, and I had been able to spruce up the President's image by taking a bit of liberty with my P.R. man's license." (*Manchester Guardian Weekly*, April 24, 1988)

What Speakes did is all part of "packaging" a politician, a practice surely regrettable but not in the same category as, for example, whatever it was that went on in the Irangate affair.[4] If people felt anything very negative about the Speakes incident, most likely it was not dismay over his creative reporting but rather regret that the country was in the hands of an old man whose already minuscule capacity for leadership was evidently diminishing fast. Oliver North and his fellows, on the other hand, perhaps deserve a more strongly negative judgment. Who did not feel insulted by the patent hypocrisy and that teary and sappy travesty of heroism put forward by Colonel North and his noisy lawyer in their defense before the Senate? But who also would claim that counter intelligence should be run on a basis of "open and honest government?" It was almost a relief to hear accusations of plain embezzlement; that, so to speak, was good honest straightforward dishonesty.

The plain truth, in fact, by which one might assess the gravity of Mr. Speakes's offense, apparently is not easy to come by in the city where he lived.

The particular kind of falsehood Mr Speakes admits to telling in his book probably didn't even seem like such a big deal to him because there is so much dissembling in this city as to who said what, and what is authentic. For years speeches that were never given were made to seem in the Congressional So-Called Record as if they had been. Ghosts write reams of prose purported to have originated with someone else. Lies are told for what unrepentant liars later say were policy reasons—and all these things are done by people who are the first to complain with enormous indignation if they are even sightly misquoted, whatever that now means. (*Manchester Guardian Weekly*, April 24, 1988)

Whose heart does not bleed for the poor Washington journalist, thirsting for the clear waters of truth in such a desert of deceit?

---

[4]This is another name for the Iran-Contra scandal.

What of the "abiding mistrust and contempt of the public" which the essay writer said belied the spirit of democracy? At first that statement sounds indisputable; lies imply that the public are not fit to be trusted with the truth. To believe that is to demean them and to show contempt for them. But that is not always the case; lies can also show respect. Until I learned that their view of the social world and its associated rhetoric were not like mine, I was puzzled and offended by polite young Indians who responded to a request by assuring me they would "do the necessary," all the time (as I realized later) having no intention of doing it. Eventually I came to learn that in their world the direct refusal of a request constitutes a forceful claim to superiority. Indeed, it suggests gross disrespect and would be near enough in our culture to saying "The hell I will! Go find some other sucker!" So the apparent false promises are not that at all; they count not as lies but rather as polite fictions that preserve someone's identity and self-respect and maintain harmonious relations. Pretense is obligatory when manifesting the truth might give offence. Nor is that habit exclusively Indian. Listen to the Parisian artist, asked by his brother to show his paintings (the brother has come to borrow money):

> Here is another exasperating characteristic of bourgeois behavior: the ritual aspect of life. What a ludicrous rite, after all, forcing me to display my canvases! Georges doesn't give a damn for what I paint; I don't give a damn for what he thinks of it; he doesn't understand the first thing about it; I derive no pleasure whatsoever from his esteem. Even so, I have never had the courage to tell him all this, as a real cynic or a Quaker would do. . . . Society is based on buffooneries concealing the absence of any genuine feeling. (Dutourd 1970:31)

This assessment must complicate the judgment that lies indicate contempt. The recipient knows what is being said is false, and the speaker knows that the recipient knows; yet they are mutually reticent. Buffoonery or not, is not the contempt then purged? That kind of collusive disregard for the truth is common in our culture, and it indicates, in this instance, that one sets a high value on the other person's self-respect and therefore on the community so formed. To complicate matters further, such collusive pretence can also be used both to assert that one values the community and, at the same time, to express an adversarial contempt for that particular partner in the community: "With all due respect . . ."

The Search: What Is Truthfulness?

Lying: Moral Choice in Public and Private Life (Bok 1979) is a book of practical ethics. Briefly, Sissela Bok says that lies can have bad consequences, that sometimes they seem to be inevitable, but we should try to avoid them. We should avoid them for much the same reasons that the writer in the *Los Angeles Times* implies: even little white lies lead to habitual disregard for truth and create a climate in which deceit prevails. In my scheme of things, some of that is true: deceit does prevail. But the implied lesson—that generally lies are to be avoided by ourselves and discouraged or punished in others—is misleading because it is based on the false assumption that lies are readily identified.

Bok makes life simpler for herself as a thinker (but not for those in search of practical guidance in ethical matters) by focusing upon what she calls "clear-cut lies." She proposes "that we remove these filters [error, self-deception, variations in intention to deceive and so on—the metaphor is optical] in the chapters that follow, so as to look primarily at clear-cut lies—lies where the intention to mislead is obvious, where the liar knows that what he is communicating is not what he believes, and where he has not deluded himself into believing his own deceits" (1979:16–17). That seems straightforward. She implies that we know when we are lying. "I'll see what can be done," we say, knowing full well that there is nothing we can or will do. Aware that we practice deceit ourselves, we infer—and surely correctly—that other people are up to the same game.

So we watch for clues; the best kind are physical and observable, proof against simulation or dissimulation. If someone tells you he has never touched alcohol in his life and his breath stinks of gin, then it seems reasonable to suppose that he is lying or perhaps is deploying a mental reservation ("Never *touched* it, just *drank* it"). But is that supposition reasonable? Might he not be so far gone into alcoholism that he is merely mistaken, by now unaware that gin is alcohol? Suppose he tells you that he drinks but does not have a drinking problem. How could anyone be sure that is deceit? Even if you find him later flat in the gutter outside a pub, that would be no proof of deceit; it could be self-misdiagnosis.

There are also behavioral clues. We look to see if she is sweating, thus applying a rough-and-ready lie-detector test. What is he doing with his eyes? Is he meeting yours? Or is he looking shiftily down at his feet? Does the voice sound natural? We can also use linguistic clues of words and style. Is she protesting too much? Is he being more theatrical than would be in character, laying his hand on his heart and loudly inviting God to strike him dead if he is telling a lie?

But are such clues clear signs of deception? She may be sweating not because she is lying but because she is afraid. Or because it is a hot day. Some people always look at the ground and not into another's eyes. There are cultures that put dangerous meanings into eye catching. There are also theatrical cultures and individuals given to ostentatious presentations of the self, but honest withal. Even worse, it may be that she knows eye catching signals truth telling, and so she is catching our eye just to hide the lies. Even worse than that, what are you to make of the person who mixes signals, the gangster smiling sweetly at you while promising to cut your throat the first chance he gets, or the sophisticated lady who makes love while reading a fashion magazine?

8

In short, the fact of intentional lying is indisputable and part of our own experience, and Bok's "clear-cut" lie is clearly *defined*, but since it involves the inner workings of other peoples' minds, it is also inherently difficult to identify. It is not even the case that we can be sure about ourselves. Are people not deceived about their own motivations and intentions? Bok agrees that self-deception goes on.

How can one recognize truth defined as intentional truthfulness when even our own intentions can be uncertain and when the intentions of others are usually inscrutable and, in the context of deceit, are deliberately camouflaged? Can one provide practical guidance on how to act in the presence of something that one cannot identify? Regrettably, these difficulties take the book out of the realm of *practical* ethics (what people in fact *can* and *do* take into account) into the philosopher's study (where one can speculate about what they *ought* to take into account, without ever finding out if they do or even could). The notion of "clearcut lies" is not so much a guide to good conduct as a label, one more weapon with which to commit rhetorical assault and battery.

The Search: A Family of Untruths

Bok's "clear-cut" lie, although very difficult to identify in practice, is clear enough as a concept. Her rough and ready definition (the liar should be aware of the falsity of what he or she is saying) provides a start, but a more detailed examination of the quite alarmingly large array of terms that cluster around "lie" gives one a strong sense of practical uncertainties. The very large number of words available in English, the uncertain gradation between them along various dimensions (particularly that of turpitude), and their consequent overlapping, partial inter-changeability, and general unclarity in use, are features that make it rhetorically easy for the same conduct to be variously called a lie, hyperbole, pretense, equivocation, normative insensitivity, distortion, flattery, disingenuousness, tactfulness, make-believe, evidence of a creative imagination, or any one of literally hundreds of other terms and phrases.[5] A brief survey of the various dimensions involved in the choice of particular terms will show how they are used to mark one or another kind of untruth.[6]

A man called Debohari, who worked for me in Bisipara and was a friend, by then the father of four young children, had once been employed as the schoolmaster in a village where his wife— then his betrothed—lived with her parents. Debohari's father was dead, and the principal sponsors who arranged this match were his "uncles," the senior men of his patrilineage. In that part of the world, even to see one's prospective bride is permitted only as a brief and highly ritualized "unveiling" at the betrothal ceremonies; to visit her or talk with her, even with a chaperon, would be grossly improper. It came to the uncles' notice that Debohari and his fiancee had not only been meeting clandestinely but had even been anticipating their future married status.[7] They hauled him over the coals, saying that was not good for the family's reputation. Debohari did not deny the charge, but he defended himself by claiming it was his fate (*karma*) to behave that way. The uncles laughed and said it would also be his fate to get into a heap more trouble with them if he didn't behave himself better.

From the way he grinned when he told me the story, it was clear that Debohari had been trying it on: that is, he did not expect his uncles to swallow the excuse and he himself did not think it valid. So perhaps he stands convicted as one of Bok's clear-cut liars—at least I *think* he may, because Debohari never actually admitted he didn't believe in his own excuse and to ask him would have been crass. Anyway, his demeanor and the

[5] I assume a similar richness exists in other languages but do not, of course, imply that the categorization of untruths will be the same in every culture.

[6] I intend this word to be without moral standing; that is, it covers what we condemn (lies), what we regret (error), and what we may enjoy (fiction).

[7] A son was born five months after the marriage.

response of his uncles seemed to make the matter perfectly clear. First, he had indeed gone farther toward premarital intimacy than was proper; second, he knew perfectly well that *karma* did not cancel the obligation to behave with propriety. Now let us see what else can be said about the incident.

First, to make an immediate jump to the river's other bank, the affair makes sense only if it is set in the context of a much larger untruth, the myth or basic lie of Hinduism which is constructed out of *karma*, *dharma*, reincarnation, the caste system, the divinity, *moksha*, and so forth.[8] Clearly this major untruth and Debohari's minor foray into creative redefinition of conduct are different matters. Ordinarily (that is, other than in polemics), we would not classify religious beliefs, myths, fantasies, or plain fiction in the same category as intentional falsehood. In doing so I am certainly not making an ontological claim (I have, for example, an open mind—and a preference—on the question of whether or not I am going to be born again). But I am insisting that there can be a ready transferability between the two kinds of intentional untruth (fiction and deceit), and that this rhetorical transferability arises from the feature common to both of them: empirical verification—or Popper's falsifiability or refutability (1980)—does not apply to either, being usually impossible in one case (deceit) and always inappropriate in the other (fiction).

The tactical significance of this inapplicability, of course, is that Debohari protected himself from being called a liar. Had he denied trysting with the girl, he risked a parade of evidence, and he risked gaining a reputation as a clear-cut liar. Invoking *karma*, he tried implicitly to ensure that the worst that could be said against him was either that he was a true-believer but in error (because *karma* does not work that way) or that he was faking religiosity and lacked neither ingenuity nor impudence. The uncles, I am sure, knew—at least by his account they behaved as if they knew—that Debohari was trying to pull the wool over their

[8]A comfortable introduction to the Hindu religion is to be found in Hopkins 1971.

eyes, shifting their attention from what he had actually done to a general proposition about individual responsibility and the genesis of behavior. Their—as I remember him indicating to me—slightly amused dismissal of his claim, shows quite clearly that they recognized this as deliberate evasion. It was not an error: in their opinion what he did fell into the category of deliberate and knowing deceit.

Was it then a clear-cut lie, Bok style? I do not think so. If Debohari had denied that he had ever encountered his betrothed, other than on the formally proper occasions, that would surely have been a clear-cut lie. In that event there would have been an air of objectivity about the issue: he would have been saying that something never happened when he knew it had happened (discounting, of course, fudges over just what "encounter" should mean). What he in fact did—invoke the principle of *karma*—pushes the whole matter over toward creativity, imagination, morally innocuous fiction. It invites an attention shift and with it an attitude shift. It changes the moral climate, because there is an implicit invitation to suspend reality testing. Fairy tales, just-so stories, myths, and legends may eventually be judged as being in bad taste or as having evil consequences, or their telling may be considered evidence of sinister motivations, but the first invitation is to make none of those judgments—and certainly not a judgment about factual accuracy—but rather to look to aesthetics, to creativity, to stop being judgmental and instead be entertained.[9] That, I think, is the point of the reported amusement of the uncles and Debohari's own amusement when told me the tale. Notice how at that stage both "deceit" and "error" have been neutralized.

---

[9]The same tendency, a cavalier—almost lighthearted—dismissal of objective truth, is found in the highly developed modern cultural performances of an American election campaign. When I first wrote this, Stuart Krieg Spencer was the "handler" charged with the Herculean task of making Senator Quayle appear "presidential." The *Los Angeles Times*, October 21, 1988, reported: "But the man who tried to make Nelson A. Rockefeller appear humble, Gerald R. Ford clever, Ronald Reagan informed and Manuel A. Noriega democratic, is not easily daunted."

This neutralization can happen, I think, only if certain other variables are appropriate. The first of these concerns consequences; the second motivations. Iago, you will remember, did not just tell a lie; he told an *odious* lie, and it was odious because its consequences were so horrendous. The question, clearly, is Who is hurt by a lie and how badly? Imagine for a moment that to protect himself Debohari had claimed that the girl had seduced him and was in any case known to be pregnant by another man; and suppose also that it was a "clear-cut" lie—he had himself been the seducer, and she was pregnant with his child, (as indeed she was) and so forth. That would have been an odious lie for the very harm it could do to the girl, to her family, to the pattern of relationships between the families, and . . . Who knows how far the damage might be spread?

Consequences are objective things; a death, a pregnancy, a broken engagement are directly experienced, not inferred. But the *seriousness* of a consequence is not objective; it is a matter of opinion. Motivations, too, are not experienced, and as I insisted, it is difficult to make inferences about them. But guesses about them enter into the calculation, along with evaluations of consequences, on a dimension that I will call "turpitude." To lie and produce disastrous consequences that one did not anticipate is bad (it is an error and indicates stupidity) but not so bad as a lie told despite accurate foreknowledge of how much damage it would do. A straightforward denial that anything improper had ever taken place, a lie told to protect the reputation of the girl and her family and the amity that existed between the two families would earn the label of "white lie." There has to be a low rating on the dimension of turpitude, before the target (that is, the person or persons being manipulated by the lie) is willing to move a message across the major divide between falsehood and fairy tale. Debohari's creativity hurt no one. The standard reverse case, where the level of turpitude is high, is provided by those public figures who divert attention from their own shortcomings and dishonesties by the use of a scapegoat—Jews, communists, wetbacks (illegal aliens), trench-coat liberals (a somewhat undistinguished contribution to the vocabulary of political abuse from the lips of Ronald Reagan), or whatever else.

Bok centers upon a single category and implicitly assumes, for the sake of argument, that a word or a deed is a thing that either is or is not a clear-cut lie. I am suggesting a different world, one not of things but of interactions that wait to have labels put on them. I focus on all those interactions that can be labeled untrue. The act or the deed is a thing, for sure, that has consequences and was motivated. But the consequences and the motivations are names affixed by parties interested in having it recognized as one or another kind of untruth. The domain of untruth is rich. There are name sets that carry with them formal penalties for deceit: perjury, fraud, libel, slander, and false witness are examples. Others indicate a notional set of distances from some standard of truth or honesty: hyperbole, exaggeration, circumvention, misrepresentation (partial and qualified departures from righteousness), as opposed to bogus, spurious, sham, counterfeit (unequivocal negations of probity). Another pair of contrasting sets would be evasion, equivocation, prevarication, disingenuousness, or even "a slip of the tongue" against the "outright lie" or the "barefaced lie." (An obvious tactic—offensive or defensive—would be to shift the definition of what has been said or done from one to the other category.)

That there is indeed (at least in English) vast scope for creative redefinition is hinted when one looks at Roget's *Thesaurus* and discovers that for each word or phrase under "veracity" there are approximately twelve listed under its opposites.

Truth has many inversions: error, deceit, lies, concealment, hypocrisy, convention, propaganda, image making, fiction, myth, fantasy, and so on. One begins to wonder if there are any "plain lies." If there are no plain lies, how can one follow Gandhi's advice not to lie under any circumstances? To do that one has not only to know what a lie is but also be able in practice to recognize it. Let us continue the search.

The Search: Syntactical Truth

If a "clear-cut lie" will not stand up on its own and be recognized, does it follow that plain truth is equally elusive? To answer that question, we have to put truthfulness (truth telling) aside and give Pilate his response, by saying what "truth" can mean.

One kind of truth seems at first sight to be plain and objective, and that is the *truth of experience*. This is not a matter of conveying information, of telling what one believes to be true, but of propositions that are proved true or false empirically. It is the "truth" used in everyday life, an empirical truth that I have said is enshrined in our *habitus*. Truth in this case is opposed not to deceit but to error. No amount of rhetoric will change the experience of being hurt if one mistakenly thinks the best way to warm one's hands on a cold morning is to stick them in the fire. Flame damages human tissue; water will not of its own accord flow uphill, and if you design your sewage system on the assumption that it will, you will have problems; if you breakfast on *Amanita phalloides*, the symptoms of poison appear after it is too late to do anything about it and you will die. Whatever your culture, whatever your language, it seems these propositions must be objectively and absolutely true. They are part of the nature of things, like it or not.

In a sense they are. That is, the events—mushroom poisoning, water flowing downhill, fire burning—are part of the nature of things. In another sense they are not, because they are not events but propositions about events. Colin Cherry calls them "layman's truth."

There is a belief amongst laymen that science purports to represent a system of absolute truth, which is furthermore wholly independent of language; that the world behaves in such and such a way according to "blind immutable laws"—forgetting that such laws are man-made and expressed in human language. Sci-

15

entific laws are not sets of rules that Nature must obey. . . . they are rules which we ourselves must accept, if we are to communicate with one another in scientific discussion. (1961:253)

That statement does not deny the truth of experience, but it does assert that *scientific* truth is not the same as the truth of experience and is relative.

"Syntactical truth" should be distinguished from experiential, factual "plain truth." A logician may set up formal rules for combining words, or other signs, into sentences and rules by which deductions, consequences or implications may be drawn. The "truth" of any such conclusion can then be stated only with references to this particular syntactical system ("true" in such and such a system). Sentences based on such invented, pure systems need have no factual, experiential truth; and deductions drawn from initial premises do not provide any information about facts. (Cherry 1961:223)

"Layman's truth" (which is also the truth claimed by politicians) does not countenance the possibility of "syntactical truth" and assumes that all truth is experiential and absolute, unconditional and unalterable. This assumption gives the word "truth" its potent rhetorical force. The demand that truth be spoken in public affairs (the layman's demand) rests not only on whatever ethical system directs those laymen but also (at least in our culture) on the notion that there is some objective truth out there which is *the* truth and therefore is an imperative, demanding attention and compliance. Cherry's layman is not comfortable with the idea of relative truth. Even the statement that two plus two equals four or the rule in the English language that plural subjects take plural verb forms are easily seen as matters of "fact" rather than of convention, because our language lets us insist that it is simply not "true" that two plus two equals five and that what is not true is also not "a fact."

If it is a fact that water flows downhill and flames damage human flesh, is it the same kind of fact when I assert that when twelve or more Americans are together on a committee, one of them will start grandstanding? My experience certainly shows that to be the case. But there is a difference: this proposition concerns people interacting with people. It is not about natural events (water flowing downhill) or about people interacting with nature (burning their hands). Furthermore, while burned flesh and water running downhill belong in nature, in the sense that what one feels (pain) or what one sees (a flow of water) does not depend on what people say, "grandstanding" is a purely cultural construct, open to dispute as to what constitutes grandstanding, and building into itself an opinion on the behavior.

Culture is like one of Cherry's syntactical systems, but vastly enlarged, variegated, and therefore formidably confusing. People communicate and interact with one another within the framework of culture but only *to some extent*. The qualification is important, and it arises because in any interaction it is not necessarily agreed which cultural rules are to be used.

Truth, to follow Cherry, is relative to the syntactical system employed. Therefore, if all parties agreed upon that system— that is, upon the premises of argument—then *within that system* truth would be regarded as "objective" and apparent to everyone. But this is often—perhaps usually—not the case with cultures. A culture enshrines values and beliefs and identifies motives and institutions and contains assertions about human nature and the human condition, but it is neither unitary nor stable. It is disturbed by internal contradictions and it is constantly in movement. Cultures emerge in human interaction and especially in argument, and they are to be seen not as firm regulations, directing conduct, but as competitive processes by which claim and counterclaim continually modify a shifting mass of propositions and directives about the way our world is and the way it should be.

The "truth" that is involved in such arguments—I have in mind political discourse—is far removed from the truth of experience. It is the kind of conditional truth that characterizes syntactical systems and is contingent on the axioms shaping that particular system. Whenever politicians claim to be in possession of *the* truth, asserting their particular truth to be objective and confirmed by experience, they are lying or are mistaken because they are of necessity dealing with a culture, being at once constrained by it and shaping it, so far as they can, according to their ambitions. They shape the culture by insisting that others make use of a particular syntactical system, perhaps one in which they sincerely believe or, if they are deceitful, one they think is rubbish but will serve their present purposes. It is this capacity to shape the other person's world by imposing one's own definitions on the situation, that makes it difficult in practice to find a firm line between truth and error or truth and deceit (or, for that matter, error and deceit).

Objective truth (truth by correspondence) and syntactical truth (truth by coherence) in the end differ only in respect of their audience. Objective truth assumes a single audience and so in effect makes audience a nonvariable: there is no one in the world, and there never will be anyone, who will not discover that it is an error to think that water flows uphill. Truth by coherence cannot be so straightforwardly described. There is not one audience, but many: different audiences, different truths. But each distinct truth gives authority to only one audience and degrades all others as being in error or in sin, deaf to the voice that is the one hope of salvation. In practical affairs truth by coherence is seldom acknowledged as syntactical and relative; when it is the product of a consensus or even of a head count, those very processes transform it into *the* truth, from which there can be no legitimate departure. This is often the case even in the natural sciences, as Kuhn (1970) and others have argued; it is always the case in politics.

If that is so, the difference between absolute truth and relative truth itself becomes relative, being no more than the ease or the frequency with which any particular truth finds itself effectively disputed. Experiential truth of the simple hands-in-the-fire kind is never going to be effectively disputed; the merits of different forms of government are always going to be disputed. Each end of the continuum is firm, but where along the line the break occurs between absolute and relative truth is undeterminable. Perhaps there are no absolute truths in politics, perhaps not in any part of culture. How true that proposition is and, if it is true, to what extent it should matter will eventually be argued. Meanwhile, we continue the search.

The Search: Truth Is Harmony

Here is an excerpt from a dialogue in 1920 between Gandhi and a counsel before the Hunter Committee.[10] It concerns satyagraha (truth-struggle). Counsel speaks first:

C: However honestly a man may strive in his search for truth, his notions of truth may be different from the notions of others. Who then is to determine the truth?
G: The individual himself would determine that.
C: Different individuals would have different views as to truth. Would that not lead to confusion?
G: I do not think so. (Bondurant 1965:20)

That bland and confident rejoinder should have provoked the counsel into asking, "What is Truth?" In fact Gandhi would have had an answer. He had on hand both the touchstone by which truth was to be known and the technique for finding it. Joan Bondurant provides a neat distillation of his views.

The objective standard by which truth can be judged is a human standard expressed in terms of human needs. . . . the element of non-violence in satyagraha is inseparable from a view of truth which takes as its criterion the needs of man. In the quest for such

[10]Lord Hunter presided over a parliamentary commission inquiring into "disturbances" in the Punjab, in the course of which soldiers had killed four hundred civilians at a rally in Amritsar.

truth, and in its propagation, it is therefore not possible, in a proper satyagraha, to inflict harm on others. In so behaving, truth itself would lose its meaning. . . . Self-suffering, the third element of satyagraha, guarantees the sincerity of the satyagrahi's own opinions, the while it restrains him from propagating uncertain truths. (1965:31,33)

That final phrase can only mean that truth is what the satyagrahi will suffer for because he is certain of the rightness of his own opinion. That potentially disturbing thought and the somewhat wishful and essentially impractical and even irresponsible element in satyagraha will be considered later. The notion is introduced here so that we can examine the axiomatic basis that underlies Gandhi's definition of truth by the criterion of human needs. This particular notion of truth has many transformations, ranging from the simple white lie to a cosmic philosophy about the nature of the universe and the people in it.

This philosophy rejects the notion of conflict, of the opposition of contradictories, as a permanent and inescapable feature of human existence. Truth is not found by analyzing and dividing and contrasting but by seeking to apprehend the whole. This belief is marked by some authorities as a feature of Eastern philosophies. Robert Oliver, for example, writes: "Whereas the West has favored analysis and division of subject matter into identifiable and separate entities, the East has believed that to see truth steadily one must see it whole" (1971:10). In other words, "The test of truth . . . is the ability to see the essential unity that inheres amidst all manner of contradictories" (1971:77). These ideas are part not only of Eastern philosophies but also of science, indeed of any knowledge, for we can understand a particular event only by rising above it to the general category in which it is located. The truth is made apparent only in a comprehensive view, in the context of a whole. A whole is, of course, an analytical simplification, an abstraction from a richer and fuller reality.

One form of comprehension which seems *not* to be the product of analysis is within everyone's experience. It happens when we sense, effortlessly and in a quite mystical and usually emotional way, the "truth" of a work of art, the poetic phrase that somehow is stronger than a treatise, the portrait that does not resemble the sitter but communicates the essence of something that a plain likeness could never convey.[11] "Poetic" truth is a truth that does not rest on analysis: of course analysis is possible and certainly people try and sometimes are convincing, but the analysis comes after the event and the event is a perfectly valid experience independent of any analysis. "Poetic" truth does not come upon the viewer as a result of reading what critics say, nor does it come step-by-step in the manner of reasoned calculation. It comes all at once, whole and entire, endowed, so to speak, with its own authority.

Close to this is coherence-truth, Cherry's syntactical truth, the kind of truth that resides in a system. One scheme of interpretation is privileged and used to mark as true or false any proposition according to whether it will fit into the system. Examples of such syntactical systems are Euclidean geometry, Marxist history, fundamentalist Christianity, even (despite what its practitioners claim) postmodernist anthropology, which is mostly an exercise in the falsification (perhaps "denigration" is a better word) of other systems.[12] The perception of a system and of where each part fits lies behind that obscure but doubly enchanting phrase "truth is beauty." One can fall in love with such systems, even postmodernism. As for Euclidean geometry, there is a wonderful account in John Aubrey's *Brief Lives* (quoted in Cherry 1961:217) of how Hobbes discovered it.

> He was 40 years old before he looked upon geometry; which happened accidentally. Being in a gentleman's library . . . Euclid's *Elements* lay open and 'twas the 47 El, libri 1. He read the Proposition. "By g*——" say'd he "this is impossible!" So he

---

[11]I am thinking of Graham Sutherland's painting of Churchill, destroyed (so it is said) by Mrs. Churchill.

[12]These strictures will be justified in Chapter 4.

read the demonstration of it, which referred him back to such a proposition; which proposition he read. That referred him back to another, which he also read. *Et sic deinceps*, that at last he was demonstratively convinced of that truth. This made him in love with geometry.

(*He would now and then sweare, by way of emphasis.)

Given "truth" and "beauty," can "harmony" be far behind? The "social need" that concerned Gandhi was indeed social: the need for mutual respect and consideration, for a harmonious society, for the elimination of competition and individual ambition. Such a society was not to be constructed, built up, so to speak, from individual components. It existed, waiting to be uncovered, to be realized, revealed in the same way that the beauty of a poem or a painting reveals itself as compelling and indisputable. The eternal verity, then, is the "essential unity" of all things, including society, including all humankind. This essential unity is seen as an objective fact, thus anchoring moral principles firmly into a bedrock of reality. From this it follows that if there is such a thing as social engineering, it can proceed only by so educating people that they accommodate themselves to that unity: "Attention should be directed away from the externals of physical problems and social ills to the internal realities of the spiritual nature and unity of all being. In other words, the goal should be to try to adjust people to circumstances, rather than to try to adjust circumstances to people" (Oliver 1971:77–78).

The practical ethics entailed in this view may be encountered also in societies where the fundamental assumption of natural harmony is not explicitly formulated or is even denied. Those small enclaves in our judicial system (mostly having to do with marital troubles) which look first to reconciliation and the restoration of the social fabric and only second to precedent and good law are an example. Indian panchayats (councils) set out to restore broken relationships or, if necessary, to end them and restore a wider harmony and, both in their procedures and in the (to us) lax way in which they enforce decisions, are mostly

unconcerned with other kinds of "truth," testamentary or factual. The white lie, as I said, is a humble realization of the same
axiom of social harmony.

So much for the touchstone of truth. Now let us consider
Gandhi's technique for arriving at it through the "truth-struggle." Essentially the technique is that of Socrates. Truth in the end
is reached when debaters exchange views, moving from thesis to
antithesis and coming together in a synthesis, thus, in the end, of
their own free will recognizing *the* truth. Rhetoric and other
forms of violence are eschewed because they impede the uncovering of truth. Gandhi "had discovered, early in his application of
satyagraha, 'that pursuit of truth did not admit of violence being
inflicted on one's opponent but that he must be weaned from
error by patience and sympathy.' 'For,' he added, 'what appears
to be truth to the one may appear to be error to the other'"
(Bondurant 1965:16). The counsel at the Hunter hearings was
evidently skeptical. So now let us ask how near in practice satyagraha came to finding truth.

The Search: Satyagraha

The link between deceit and coercive power is often
noted. Princes rule by force or by fraud, Machiavelli said, and
fraud is the more efficient instrument: "I believe it to be most true
that it seldom happens that men rise from low condition to high
rank without employing either force or fraud.... Nor do I believe
that force alone will ever be found to suffice, while it will often be
the case that cunning alone serves the purpose" (1950:318).
Sometimes deceit and coercion are seen as equivalent. Lies and
democracy, said the *Los Angeles Times essayist*, are incompatible, because to lie to people is to deprive them of information, to
cut down the range of their options, and thus to coerce them.
Gandhi's satyagraha—truth-struggle—eliminated lying because
lying is a form of coercion.

To define coercion out of a confrontation is at the same time to eliminate power and so make it not a confrontation but a cooperative endeavor. Ideal satyagrahis, accordingly, are not trying to enforce their will, not even trying to persuade, but rather acting from a position where the search for truth neutralizes power differences. They put these differences outside the frame of the debate. We seem to have arrived at a kind of scientific objectivity, a world where truth stands on its own and is unaffected by the status, high or low, or the ambitions of those who utter it or search for it. Neutralizing power is a precondition for attaining truth.[13] That, I think, is the essence of satyagraha, as it is also the essence of a "value-free" science.

Much that is familiar emerges in this philosophy, confused and confusing though it sounds. The affinities with Ben Franklin and with American pragmatism are clear enough: beliefs are to be accepted as true when their effects are wholesome. There is also, as I note elsewhere, a distinctly Socratic air about the dialectical endeavors of the satyagrahi and his partner. They do not argue to persuade each other: they are partners in the quest for truth. Furthermore, as Bondurant reminds us, Gandhi saw himself as "experimenting with truth"; he was dealing with praxis, with "applied ethics." But remember also that Gandhi was not merely a "saint," as sometimes is said. He was also a formidable politician.[14]

So it is appropriate to ask how things worked out in practice. When put into action, is it really the case that satyagraha neutralized or eliminated power? Did Gandhi succeed where Socrates failed? As everyone knows, these encounters were *planned*

---

[13]A somewhat similar sentiment—that the search for truth is impeded by recognition of status—is manifested in certain procedures thought to further the discovery of truth (in the sense of "new scientific knowledge"). "Brainstorming" sessions in some kinds of research teams are structured so that neither seniority nor specialization will interfere with creativity. The slightly frenetic atmosphere that results is well caught in a book about designing computers (Kidder 1981).

[14]I heard a BBC radio program of recollections and opinions about the Mahatma. From Dr. Ambedkar: "That man was no saint! He was a rascal!"

to be conspicuously nonviolent, at least from the side of the agrahis. When the police set about beating them with *lathis*,[15] the satyagrahis did not fight back or even try to protect themselves.

Notice first that these street encounters are somewhat removed from the places where dialecticians usually search for truth. Words did not much feature in them; statements emerged from deeds and the unspoken rhetoric had a great deal to do with status. Saints and martyrs lay bruised and bleeding (but undefeated) before the agents of brutal coercion. Virtue was conspicuously monopolized by one side. Was this a search for truth or was it a struggle for power, morality having become a potent weapon for the otherwise weak? Were status and power and political ambition really in abeyance?

Even if we shift the scene from the streets to peaceful encounters between debaters, in Gandhi's own scenario the strong-arm tactics of his morality are still apparent. For a proper satyagrahi in a debate, "holding to the truth means holding to what the satyagrahi believes to be the truth until he is dissuaded from that position." (Bondurant 1965:33). Satyagrahis, disclaimers notwithstanding, look rather like true-believers in themselves and in their cause. If truth is whatever debaters in the end agree is the truth, whoever holds out the longest is ipso facto demonstrated to have had the handle on truth. I cannot see this as anything but plain obstinacy, as persuasion, moral intimidation, a nonviolent form of violence in which weakness is crushed. Gandhi was invariably gentle and courteous, Nehru said, but sometimes talking to him was like "addressing a closed door" (Moraes 1973:173). Is this not a form of untruth, at least of self-deception? Satyagraha encounters, whether in debate or in the streets, did not show *minds* searching for a truth—an eternal verity that stands above and beyond the contestants—but *wills* struggling to define situations, each to the other's political disadvantage.

There is one other feature of satyagraha that brings Gandhi's

[15]An iron-bound staff used by police in India.

philosophy to the edge of hypocrisy. A dozen or perhaps even a score of highly motivated volunteers may be disciplined enough to stage a nonviolent encounter with authorities who are prone to violence; any blood that is shed is, so to speak, their own volunteered blood. But to stage a performance like that in an Indian city and pretend that there will be no violence except for police beating satyagrahis is not realistic.[16] To provoke conflict situations in which ten thousand people are supposed to congregate "nonviolently" is a practical contradiction; and Gandhi was a practical moralist. Of course that does not convict him of hypocrisy; he may merely have been deluding himself.

Whatever Gandhi's motivations and, from time to time, misgivings, the consequences were clear enough, and there can be little doubt about motivations in the case of some of those who followed him into techniques of "nonviolent" encounter with authorities. I had a conversation with an extremely active political aspirant in the late 1950s (more than a decade after Gandhi's assassination, when India was, of course, independent) about the appropriately nonviolent manner in which to provoke a "police firing" so as to acquire a martyr or two for the cause and put the authorities into an ethical doghouse—surely an ironic and unfortunate legacy of the "struggle for truth!"

The Search: Dialectic and Rhetoric

A dialectical procedure requires one to state a thesis, oppose it with an antithesis, and then work on the two like a botanist, mating the truth in each of them, so as to produce a new and better strain, a synthesis. That synthesis itself becomes a thesis for a new cycle, and so on until *the* truth emerges. One

[16]I have in my notes a cutting from a Calcutta newspaper in 1959, reporting a riot in which twenty people lost their lives. It began with an argument over the price of a banana.

knows when one has reached that point, because the debaters agree that they have found the truth.

Debates, especially on public affairs, do have exactly that tendency to fly toward opposites: liberty versus discipline; the individual versus the collectivity; capitalism versus socialism; reason versus the passions; and truth versus deceit. Let us then reconstruct my argument in dialectical form.

The opening thesis (truth) is the one embraced by Bok and many others: *Society is better if truth telling prevails as the rule in public and private affairs.* The antithesis must concern truth's opposites: either error or deceit. Since it is nonsense to claim that society will benefit if error prevails, we are left with Bok's deceit—deliberate concealing of what one knows to be the case or deliberate promotion of what one knows not to be true. *Society requires for its survival the practice of deceit.* Bok accepts this proposition, somewhat reluctantly, and so, with varying degrees of cynicism, do many other authorities.

Here is Francis Bacon, presenting human nature as he saw it, not, presumably, as he thought it ought to be:

Certainly the ablest of men that ever were have had all an openness and frankness of dealing; and a name of certainty and veracity; but they were like horses well-managed; for they could tell passing well when to stop or turn; and at such times when they thought the case indeed required dissimulation, if then they used it, it came to pass that the former opinion spread abroad of their good name and clearness of dealing made them almost invisible. (1909:18)

In other words, one of the benefits of being known to tell the truth is that when you do come to lie, people believe you.

Bacon, like Bok and most others, regrets the need to be less than honest: "The best composition and temperature [temperament] is to have an openness in fame and opinion; secrecy in habit; dissimulation in seasonable use; and a power to feign if there be no remedy" (1909:20). The reason why dishonesty is inevitable is given by Machiavelli in a famous sentence: "A man who wishes to make a profession of goodness in everything must necessarily come to grief among so many who are not good" (1950:56).

The heart of the matter, evidently, is the exercise of power. I will come to that later. Meanwhile the antithesis is stated in the clearest of terms, this time in Plato's *Republic*: "If anyone, then, is to practice deception, either on the country's enemies or on its citizens, it must be the Rulers of the commonwealth, acting for its benefit; no one else may meddle with this privilege" (Cornford 1981:78).[17]

The thesis and the antithesis take the form of opposing what ought to be with what is: truth should always prevail, but deceit is not only present but also necessary. What form does the synthesis ("putting together") take? In the practice of politics it is not what is usually considered to be a synthesis. It is not a constructive amalgamation, not the breeding of a new strain of truth; it is a fight. This fight is not Milton's grand allegory of the struggle between the forces of good and evil but a more everyday affair, a conflict between adversaries intent on demonstrating that their own "syntactical system" contains *the* truth and is therefore good, whereas the rival scheme is mere deceit and therefore evil.

Obviously this is not a resolution that can become a new thesis. It is a conflict that continues until resolved by means *other than reason*. Whatever Socrates and Gandhi may stipulate, struggles of this kind are not conducted through the dialectic. There is no invitation to reason from opposite to opposite so as to arrive at a

[17]Having an eye on rhetoric, it is worth noticing a slight difference between this translation and that of Popper (1980:1.138): "It is the business of the rulers of the city, if it is anybody's, to tell lies, deceiving both its enemies and its own citizens for the benefit of the city; and no one else must touch this privilege." The conditional clause is buried by Popper's placing of it. Cornford's version, opening with the conditional clause, highlights the sentiment that untruthfulness in general is to be avoided if possible, and picks up a statement in the preceding paragraph; "Again, a high value must be set upon truthfulness." Popper, rooting for the "open society," highlights the lie.

new truth but, rather, plain assertions fortified by rhetoric, less an exercise of reason than a butting of heads. It is a fight to define a situation. What purports to be a search for truth through the dialectical process is in reality an effort to dominate by persuasion. In practice the argument is "resolved" either when one side succeeds in intimidating the other or when circumstances force a compromise (neither side can sufficiently intimidate the other and a decision cannot wait). The dialectic that goes on evenhandedly and without mutual manipulation or intimidation is a philosopher's luxury (or perhaps a philosopher's fantasy). Certainly it is denied to a politician or anyone acting on the world. Life in society involves power, and power involves persuasion, and persuasion in practical affairs where interests are at stake is not determined by dialectical reasoning, by logic, but by its false equivalent, rhetoric. Rhetoric, moreover, is a form of deceit.

> The goal of rhetoric . . . is the power to persuade (*peithein*) others, to reduce them to one's will. The goal of the dialectic is the opposite of persuasion: it is to be refuted (*elenchestai*), humiliated, corrected. This means that rhetoric naturally treats others as means to an end, while dialectic treats them as ends in themselves. Rhetoric persuades another not by refuting but by flattering him, by appealing to what pleases rather than to what is best for him; if successful, it therefore injures him. [But dialectic] is not a competition to see who can reduce the other to his will; it is a process of mutual discovery and mutual refutation. One accepts refutation gladly, for it reduces the divisions and disharmonies within the self. (White 1984:110)

It takes a good person to "accept refutation gladly," and ordinary Jill and ordinary Joe usually feel better about themselves when they win an argument. The very word *compromise* carries with it overtones of the coward who lacks principle and betrays the truth. White is discussing the *Gorgias* in the passage just quoted, and he goes on to point out that in fact Socrates never managed, at least in the *Gorgias*, to make the dialectical process work. His opponents, so far from coming to agree with him upon the truth, were reduced to confused hostility or baffled silence. The dialectical process, like "truth" itself, has then become nothing more than another weapon in the armory of rhetoric. Gandhi's struggle to make truth prevail, satyagraha, turned out in just that same way, as we saw.

Everyman's Truth

Whatever be our philosophical views (if we have any on this question), we surely conduct much of our lives as nominalists (Bourdieu's hidden part of culture notwithstanding). We pretend that things to which we have not given a name do not exist (or at least that we need not notice their existence). Alternatively, if any particular phenomenon is noticed, its nature (and therefore the expected consequences that will flow from having one kind of nature rather than another) is determined *for us* by the label that comes attached to the phenomenon. If the curry is "Madras," then it is going to be hot.

Not every one finds the same label attached to the "same" phenomenon. The same curry that is bland in Madras produces heartburn in the Punjab. What I see as earthshaking, you may see as a storm in a teacup. My hero is your villain, and the lady whom others esteem as a nurturant and kindly mother, her children experience as an overpossessive dominating ogre. More things than beauty are in the eye of the beholder.

Most people are comfortable with that trite sentiment, when it concerns beauty. They are less at ease with the notion that goodness likewise is subjective, a matter of opinion. They also feel anxious when they encounter otherwise normal people who live with a definition of reality that is patently out of line with what *qualified* people (such as themselves) define as the objective truth. The flat-earther who happens also to be a good neighbor and a regular guy is a bit of a wonder. They are even more shaken if they are told that what *they themselves* see as part of an objective and undeniable world—perhaps their own sterling character—is not seen that way by other people and in truth may be nothing more than a "foolish notion."[18]

Ordinary people are disturbed by the idea that there may be no absolute and objective truth. We live our everyday lives in the posture of empiricists: we insist there is a real world "out there," and you can go out and see it or hear it or in some other way experience it and use this experience to test the truth of propositions. Even if that kind of empirical testing is impossible, because the events were in the past and the record is incomplete—just exactly what time of day did Caesar in person cross the Rubicon?—we still believe that objectively there was a particular time of day for his crossing and that that particular time would constitute *the* true answer to the question. More than that, in a somewhat confused way we see truth itself as existing out there in the world, absolute and readily recognizable—a plain truth that is opposed to opinion and error and deceit. For most people this itself is not a matter of opinion, what Bourdieu (1982) calls *doxa*, but is embedded in the *habitus,* that part of culture which is taken for granted. People need (or think they need) *truth* at the center; if not, things fall apart.

Nevertheless, these same ordinary people, while insisting on the existence and accessibility of an absolute truth, do not always use it to regulate their lives. They behave as if truth were relative to context: they tell white lies, or they adjust the level of explanation for some action or event to the perceived sophistication of their audience. The technical expertise that experts trade with one another is not what they produce for journalists or senators or even funding agencies. We do it all the time. Adolescents, we believe, have come to the age when they are entitled to know *the* truth (not fantasies) about the biology of procreation. But for little children we have simple and charming stories about the stork or how babies are found under gooseberry bushes.

---

[18]"O wad some Pow'r the giftie gie us / To see oursels as others see us! / It wad frae mony a blunder free us, / And foolish notion" (Robert Burns, "To a Louse").

Pretense is all around us and takes many forms. Goffman politely and comprehensively speaks of "selective inattention and suppression" (1961:62). In its active form this is "impression management" (1959:208)—showing to the world only those parts of one's self that one thinks desirable or proper or politic. Passively it appears as "civil inattention" (1966:83)—the etiquette that requires one not to notice features in others that might cause embarrassment.

This same capacity to disregard known attributes is also the essence of bureaucracy: individuals are reduced—defined down to—a set of features limited to the needs of the bureaucratic process. A bureaucracy deals with composite nonpersons, and much knowledge that is available is, by design and of necessity, left unused (providing, of course, that everyone is behaving with bureaucratic propriety).

Something similar is true of rituals and ceremonies and performances in general. These are successful to the extent that everyone concerned—actors and audience—tacitly suspend the reality-testing apparatus through which they try to conduct everyday affairs. If someone points out loudly that the emperor has no clothes or that Peter Pan has a bigger bust than Wendy, the charm—the magic—of the performance is in danger of being lost.[19]

The same phenomenon appears in Bateson's "framing" (1972:184). Putting a frame around an interaction constitutes a metamessage (a rule) that knowledge normally called up by items of information when *outside* the frame, *within* the frame should be disregarded. A bite within the frame of play does not signal its usual hostility; it is only pretense. The rules of the game say that since this is play, the convention that equates a bite with aggression is suspended. Pay attention to what is in the frame and,

[19]The reference is not directly to J. M. Barrie's book, and certainly not to the ingenious Freudian interpretations that have been offered of the relationship between Peter Pan and Wendy, but to the simple Christmas pantomime performances of my childhood, in which Peter Pan (played by a woman in tights and a Robin Hood tunic) courted Wendy (played by a woman in a long frilly skirt).

although you know perfectly well what the meaning would be outside, disregard it.[20]

The matter is cogently stated by Georg Simmel in his discussion of secrecy: "We simply cannot imagine an interaction or a social relation or a society which is *not* based on this teleologically determined non-knowledge of one another" (1964:312). Cooperative interaction, in other words, depends upon designedly imperfect knowledge, the result of collusion or secrecy or deception: some facts must be treated as if they were not facts. Of course, total knowledge of another person—total knowledge of anything at all—is an impossibility. But that is not the point: rather it is the deliberate engineering of "non-knowledge," which arises not only from ignorance and from deception but also from *agreeing to ignore* what is known. Knowledge that is treated as if it were secret, though in fact it is known, is an "open secret."

To have knowledge of other persons is potentially to have power over them. The matter, of course, is relative. To know that they are very strong and could without much effort tear you limb from limb does not give you control over them, but at least you can better avoid accidental dismemberment. To know something about them that they do not know or do not know that you know, is a distinct tactical advantage because you can anticipate their reactions and movements, while they do not know that you have this capacity. Indeed, *any* relevant knowledge gives potential power, especially if the other person does not have it. In other words, a secret is a form of political capital that can be invested in domination or in resisting domination by others.

That being so, *open* secrets indicate an agreement, voluntary or involuntary, *not* to make such an investment. The emperor's nakedness is seen but not mentioned; his definition of the situation is allowed to prevail and is *publicly* accepted. Peter Pan's all-too-obvious pointers to gender go ostensibly unnoticed and s/he

---

[20]The matter is not so simple. A bite, including a love bite, is not a kiss, and the connotations that the frame orders disregarded continue marginally in being and leave open possibilities for subsequent political use. The frame, to mix a metaphor, is porous.

may make a play for Wendy without seeming to manifest unnatural tendencies. The agreement is usually tacit, presumably because it is difficult to make open reference to an open secret without making it a nonsecret.

It is not only a matter of the strong imposing "truth" on the weak. Much of our untruthful "reality" is voluntary make-believe; the world can be the world of the beholder, what Ibsen in *The Wild Duck* called "life's lie," the simplified and (sometimes) comforting reinterpretation of our experience. We pretend that the world is how we wish it to be, and we are likely to make our plans as if the world really were that way. It sounds like a recipe for disaster, and sometimes it turns out to be so. But, I will argue, matters could not be otherwise. Individuals could not survive emotionally or cognitively without the solace and intellectual convenience of a simplified representation of their world, which gives them the feeling that to some extent they understand and therefore control their lives.

My argument will go further. Psychological needs aside, a *social* world without pretense, without a perfectly knowing refabrication of what is thought to be reality, would be an impossibility. Everyman's truth is what he and others negotiate it to be.

2 | Collusive Lying

> The Social Contract is nothing more than a vast conspiracy of
> human beings to lie and humbug themselves and one another
> for the general Good.
> > —H. G. Wells, *Love and Mr. Lewisham*

Primal Consensus

Collusive lying occurs when two parties, knowing full
well that what they are saying or doing is false, collude in ignoring the falsity. They hold it between them as an open secret. They
may do so voluntarily or because one party compels the other to
go along with the pretense. What they sustain is the collective and
conscious variant of "life's lie."[1] That the lie is conscious either
has to be inferred from an apparent failure to notice something
that in that particular culture is transparently obvious,[2] or is

---

[1]The psychological status of a *personal* basic lie—to what extent it is con-
sciously held—is hard to determine. Ibsen's play insists that to confront someone with his "life's lie" and make it explicit, is to risk causing a nervous
breakdown, which suggests that the falsity is not part of consciousness. But there
are other indications that the element of fantasy and wishful thinking is suppressed rather than deeply repressed into the unconscious and that simple
negative experiences may bring its falsity into consciousness. One detects, in
other words, an element of calculation in the construction of personal basic lies.
Alternatively, moving toward sociology, they are more appropriately seen as
part of the *habitus* rather than of a Freudian unconscious.

[2]Reading the "transparently obvious" across cultures is not a simple matter.

revealed when the parties divulge in private (that is, before a restricted audience) what in public had been concealed or when, under challenge, they "correct" it. An example, highly structured, will make all these statements clear.

The celebration of a marriage in many parts of the world is an occasion for expressing hostility between the bride's people (family and sometimes community) and the groom's people. The bride's people erect barriers and exact penalties, while the groom's side conducts itself like a fighting patrol out to capture a prisoner.

All this is nicely symbolized in the formal speeches that are made when the boy's people in the Kond Hills go to the girl's village to hand over the bridewealth.[3] The two parties sit facing each other, and then the bride's spokesman opens the proceedings by proclaiming that, seeing the "big turbans and strong arms" of the visitors, they are afraid. "From what country do you come?" he asks. "From far away," the groom's orator replies and then launches into an elaborate account of how they chanced by this place and saw in the pool a lotus of surpassing beauty, which they have a mind to pluck and take with them. The bride's spokesman replies that many others have tried to pluck the flower but have gone away in fear because the pool is very deep and contains fierce crocodiles and dangerous serpents. Then the groom's orator says they have a well-built boat with them, as it happens, and weapons to slay the crocodiles and medicine to counter the snakes' poison, and come what may, they will pluck the flower.

They continue in this fashion, negotiating by the familiar device of mutual intimidation, and then they pass to bargaining. "The price of that flower," the bride's party says, "is beyond pricing. But if the gold and silver that you bring stand as tall as the flower, then you may take it." The groom's spokesman replies, "Whatever be the price, we will pay it."

[3]The Kond Hills lie in western central Orissa, India, south of the Mahanadi River. About five in every eight persons are Konds; the rest are Oriyas. The speeches recorded here were provided by an Oriya informant of the Warrior caste and reflect the customs of that caste. See Bailey 1957 and 1960.

Then, the conventions having been duly observed, there is an abrupt shift from poetry to business, and the bride's representative says, "Then fetch it out and let's get it counted!" and that is what they then do.[4]

This highly stylized exchange constitutes one in a series of episodes that go to make a marriage. The scene that I described is a symbolic acting-out of combat, followed by reconciliation and cooperation. Other more private and less ceremonial negotiations had already taken place and agreement had been reached before the public display was allowed to happen. The race had been fixed, so to speak, off the course.

A go-between had been at work, conveying discreet inquiries by both parties about the temperament of the bride and the groom and the financial standing of their respective families and other delicate matters. One or more private meetings had been held between representatives of the two families, in the course of which a behind-the-scenes settlement of what in fact would go into the bridewealth and into the dowry had been concluded. Things often fall apart in these private negotiations, but because they are ostensibly private no one is supposed to lose face.[5] The prospect of losing face is, of course, apt to arouse nonrealistic sentiments, and a man can be moved to cut off his nose to save his face.[6]

---

[4]The traffic, of course, is not in gold or silver but in rupees. The amount is fixed by the custom of the caste involved, although at that time there were frequent complaints in caste councils that unscrupulous families were bidding up the price beyond what was proper.

[5]The negotiations are in fact never *entirely* private, and there is likely to be gossip, especially when they fall apart. But (providing everyone follows the rules) the performers are protected because there is another act of collusive pretense: that the negotiations are private and not available for *public* comment and political use.

[6]Realistic conflict is that in which the contest is a means to some further end, the notion being that if some better way of achieving this end than having a fight is identified, the contestants will come to a compromise. Nonrealistic conflict, by contrast, is a contest that has become an end in itself, and nothing counts except victory over the opponent. The implication is that if some well-meaning third party "resolves" the latter kind of conflict, the contestants will look around for another issue over which to continue the fight. See Coser 1956.

The ceremony is a lie. I do not mean merely that there are no snakes and no crocodiles and no boats and no heaps of gold and silver. The ceremony itself is false in the sense that it is like the facade on a building, presenting to the beholder a front that is more acceptable than the real building that it conceals. But at the same time, since everyone knows the nature of the real building, it is as if the architect has been at pains to conceal the lie and to make the facade plausible: a prison should look somewhat like a prison and not like a pleasure dome. Let us see how near the wedding-speech performance in the Kond Hills comes to the underlying reality.

One might expect, since everything has been arranged behind the scenes, that the public ceremonial would resemble speeches that are customary at a wedding breakfast in England—rejoicing and mutual congratulations and the anticipatory celebration of blessings to come.[7] Instead, it is a tale of conflict, running through the stages of confrontation (challenges and attempts at mutual intimidation) and encounter[8] (striking the bargain). The hostility is somewhat ponderously symbolized. The groom's people are presented as strangers from a far country, almost marauders, wandering the land in search of a prize. The bride's people have the prize but are reluctant to part with it. The antagonists negotiate by rattling sabers: big arms and big turbans and crocodiles and snakes and so forth. Then they strike a bargain, the "buyers" agreeing to give what the "sellers" are asking.

Why should they symbolize[9] their past antagonisms? It could

[7]They are not always so bland, even in England. I recall an occasion on which the bride's father, carefully looking away from his daughter's mother-in-law, made it elegantly clear (but in veiled and indirect words) that there had already been too much in-law interference and that the couples' happiness depended upon being given room to make their own lives. Open secrets lie around waiting to be used by those who know how to do so.

[8]This word signifies a clear and undisputed outcome to a conflict. "Confrontation" is a challenge. See Bailey 1969:28–30.

[9]The performance is obviously rich in a variety of symbols that might be discussed—snakes and the plucking of flowers and openings with teeth in them and so forth. I confine myself to those symbols that seem directly to concern social or interpersonal (not intrapsychic) conflict.

be a ritual celebration of immunity, a mock reexposure to hostility that is now without risk. That is a possibility. Another interpretation (not incompatible with the first) better suits my present argument. The ceremony rewrites the history of the marriage negotiations in a form that not only is memorable (because it is both dramatic and stylized) but also is a preemptive exclusion from the *public* record (but not from *all* records) of what in fact had happened. In that sense the ceremony is a falsification. I am reminded of university committees: two hours of acrimonious argument appear in the minutes as "After some discussion, it was agreed . . ." The infuriated adversaries and their truculence disappear from the *official* history in that phrase "after some discussion."

Indeed, even if the fact of conflict itself is memorialized in the wedding rituals, the contestants and their detailed claims and counterclaims are not. As persons (and still more decisively as individuals) they vanish behind a screen of indirect speaking, metaphors about lotus flowers and crocodiles and snakes. The—sometimes—months of prior negotiation are swept under the rug by the pretense that these are strangers meeting for the first time. The itemized agreements that have emerged from prior bargaining over brideprice and dowry (and that have been recorded, often written down and witnessed) are simplified into the token form of a pile of gold and silver as tall as is the bride. The rich antagonisms of real life are stylized out of the "official" record.

In short, there is in the performance that kind of rationality which is constructed after the event, after chaos, to make it seem that what was done haphazardly and confrontationally was really cooperative and guided by reason. There is a collusive fiction that the past was different from what all concerned know it in fact was, and both parties manipulate the "facts" into a form that they evidently think will be to their mutual advantage. The fiction thus preserved is that life is orderly, structured, predictable, and under control.

Now look at another case, also, as it happens, a wedding, but centered upon issues of another kind and much less structured.

The occasion is an actual wedding in the Kond Hills in a village called Baderi.[10] Marriage parties bring with them musicians who are untouchables. The visitors and their musicians, together with certain people from the host village, are feasted, the untouchables sitting apart from the clean castes (in this village almost all Konds, the untouchables being of the Pan caste). On this occasion a mob of local Pans, not just musicians (who have a customary right to be fed) but many others too, sat down to the feast. An important man in the village, a Kond named Liringa, loudly scolded them and sent them away. Later that night, while everyone slept, the Baderi untouchables slashed the drums of the visiting musicians,[11] an act which prompted angry complaints. The Pans were then summoned to a panchayat to give an account of themselves.[12] At that meeting there was a further confrontation between them and Liringa, culminating when one Pan did something unheard-of: in full view of everyone around, he clouted Liringa across the face (which is like choosing the courtroom as the place to assault a judge).[13]

Liringa, humiliated and cross, called another meeting and persuaded the Konds to announce formally that they would terminate not only the ceremonial privileges of their untouchables (mostly playing music at weddings, being feasted and paid for the

[10]A version of this case is to be found also in Gluckman 1964.

[11]I cannot explain why they were the victims. It may be that they had shown insufficient solidarity with the Baderi untouchables. Alternatively—and very likely—the latter were drunk and had no clear motivation beyond that of embarrassing their Kond masters.

[12]Like their Oriya neighbors Konds do not admit untouchables to panchayat deliberations. Pans may bring their disputes to be settled or may bring complaints against others (including Konds), but they are not themselves members of the panchayat.

[13]The Konds are a tribal people—in India they are called *adibasis* ("original settlers")—and how closely *adibasis* are tied into Hinduism has been a matter of debate. On this occasion, however, one must see the events against the background of Hindu ideas on pollution. The Pans are untouchables: they do not marry with Konds, nor do Konds accept food and water from them, and their touch is considered polluting for a Kond. The blow is more than simply an assault; it is also a ritual affront.

performance) but also the jobs they had working as field laborers for the Konds. As it happened, this was the hot season (this is also the marriage season), and there was no farm work to be done. But when the monsoon broke in June and cultivating began, there was no sign of the lockout, and work went on normally. The incident apparently had ended itself not through negotiation or bargaining but by each side tacitly walking away.

There is a clear difference between these events and the sequence of wedding episodes. Each subsequent episode in Baderi does not rewrite past events and bury them in the past. Far from it; there are challenges and counterchallenges, confrontations that do not end in agreement, a very visible process of escalation. The *sequence* is not conventionalized;[14] it is unintended, unplanned, and for most of those concerned distinctly unnerving. It is an intrusion of nature, of the jungle, rather than a cultural performance, not pantomimed hostility, as in the wedding speeches, but a real fight. Then how did they come to make that single sweeping collusive act in which past (and very public) violence was erased from the record?

Let us first see how each party chose to define the truth of the situation. The Baderi Pans, who were driven away from the wedding feast by Liringa, were claiming to be dependents with the right to be fed on ceremonial occasions by their Kond masters. The situation should be defined, their behavior says, in the traditional idiom in which Konds are the landowners, while Pans are what Oriyas call *praja*, subjects in a quasi-familial relationship with their masters.[15]

They were joined in this view by the village headman, Ponga, at first sight an unlikely ally. He had been visiting relatives when the troubles broke out and did not return to Baderi in time to take part in the panchayat discussions. He went around boasting—to

[14]The particular confrontations (for example, an untouchable striking a Kond) do of course carry a conventional meaning.

[15]This is not a market structure; Pans are not employees to be laid off when times are hard. They are family retainers having the duties and privileges that go along with household membership.

others but not to Liringa—that if he had been at the wedding there would have been no trouble. The Pans, he said, respected him; he could have handled everything. Thus he too invoked the tradition of lord and retainer and in effect asserted that the system worked well for those who knew how to handle it. The problem, he said with some glee, was Liringa, hot-tempered, impetuous, overassertive, and, furthermore, with designs on the headmanship.[16] Liringa was the main problem, not the Pans.

Liringa also got the blame, but for different reasons, in another definition of the situation. This came from the village schoolmaster (the same Debohari whose premarital adventures came up earlier). Liringa, suffering not only from public humiliation but also from a setback to his ambitions (Debohari said), had driven his fellow Konds into announcing an absurd and unrealistic lockout. The obstreperousness of the untouchables at the wedding was just the tip of something much bigger. The fact was that Pans in Baderi had grown too numerous to be supported as field laborers, and this overpopulation had coincided with the Gandhi-inspired campaign to abolish untouchability. The same thing had been happening in Bisipara. There too the clean castes had taken action against their Pans by discharging them from their traditional *ceremonial* privileges. But the landowners of Bisipara had not been so crazy as to deprive themselves of the indispensable services of their farm laborers.

The schoolmaster's diagnosis was correct—that is, it coincided with my definition of the situation. Both in Bisipara and to a lesser extent in Baderi capitalism was on the way to replacing the

---

[16]Liringa, one of my main informants, did have such designs. His version of the genealogy that contained most of the male Kond inhabitants of the village showed his own lineage as the senior branch and Ponga's branch as descended from a man who had in the distant past turned up one day as a refugee, bearing the stigmata of someone destined for human sacrifice. Information of this kind, being insulting to peoples' ancestry, has the status of an open secret. It would be bad manners to bring it out in public. People were no less discreet about the relative seniority of the four main branches of the lineage, all presenting their own as senior but doing so in private or, if others were present, using some disclaimer such as "At least that is what I was told."

traditional feudal structure of the caste system. Land was bought and sold and labor had become a commodity. The institution of feudal retainers had lost both its economic foundation and the stabilizing effect of the concentration of force in the hands of the dominant castes.

In fact the troubled wedding and its aftermath are an episode in an agrarian conflict that began long before Gandhi's agitations against untouchability. Baderi and other villages in the region have a history of sporadic agrarian violence, breaking out when laborers could not support their families. There were tales in Baderi about a somewhat imperfect Robin Hood character, one of their own Pans, who led a band of outlaws, robbing the rich but not, it seems, having much to spare for the poor. He flourished for a few years until captured sometime in the last quarter of the nineteenth century.[17]

Such tales, together with the recent events in neighboring Bisipara, probably inclined the Konds to listen to Liringa—a persuasive speaker—and formally resolve not to employ their Pans. Liringa's definition of the situation, at least as implied in this action, did not recognize the economic revolution (to that extent he was in agreement both with Ponga and with the Pans). For Liringa the problem was one of discipline; the Pans had to be taught a lesson. Had they not violated, in the most blatant fashion, the rule of untouchability? The lesson could not be taught by violence, as in the past, because the police would interfere, and in any case there were a lot of muscular Pans around. Therefore it must be done by depriving them of their livelihood. The fact that Konds too would go hungry if the fields were not worked was discarded into the limbo of Liringa's personal (and in this instance temporary) life's lie, along with his ambitions for the headmanship and his awareness of the agrarian revolution going

[17]He was captured by "Ollenbach Saheb"—a wily sub-divisional officer whose deeds ornament the folklore of the region. Ollenbach heard that the outlaws planned to attend a wedding in Baderi and, on the quiet, provided pots and pots of country liquor. The guests drank themselves into a stupor and in the morning Ollenbach came along and carted them off to prison.

on in the region (he was indeed aware—we had on other occasions talked about it).

Thus there were several issues and it was not initially clear which was dominant. Each party, so to speak, used its own version of the agenda, implicitly and sometimes explicitly marking other versions as falsifications. There seem, then, to be several reasons not to expect a collusive version of the truth to emerge from this affair. Given competing definitions of the situation, compromise is less likely, because it is not clear what exactly is to be negotiated. Second, information erupts out of control, and then has somehow to be pushed into the domain of open secrets. Third, I heard nothing about any formal attempt to clean up the Baderi situation and put a veneer of harmony over it. But in the end the episode closed without further violence and without further public discussion.

Not all dissensions are settled like that. Sometimes people behave the way therapists tell them, grasp the nettle of what they believe to be the truth, and say what is on their mind, bringing all their anxieties and suspicions out into the open. But the Baderi people on this occasion certainly did not put all that they knew or felt into the public domain. They solved their problem—for the time being—by doing just the opposite.

The reason for the settlement is obvious: immediate necessity. The Baderi wedding was in April or May and cultivation starts around mid-June when the monsoon breaks; so there was time for tempers to cool and people to reflect. "They came to their senses," Debohari said. Both sides looked at the bottom line and decided that the harvest counted for more than Liringa's *amour propre* or a symbolic assertion about power.

The mechanism for achieving settlement also was obvious: collusive pretense. Not only the formal panchayat resolution but also the dramatic and highly public confrontations that preceded it were tacitly excluded from public discourse, put down to the level of gossip and stories told behind the hand. Only the headman's gleeful commentary on Liringa's flat feet brought partially onto the front stage a side issue, which in the end served as a convenient and plausible excuse for ignoring the dominant issue.

But why could they not have been open about it? The answer goes beneath plain material interests to two basic lies on which Kond society, in that particular form, rested.

The first is the lie of Kond brotherhood. Konds quarrel among themselves all the time but say it is deplorable to do so and strive always for public consensus. The second is the lie of Kond status in the caste system. Sacking the Pans would be not merely a gesture that had immediate economic costs but also one that was politically and emotionally perilous. The central hazard was—stretching the term a little—"revolution." Between Gandhian propaganda and the failure of the traditional patron-client system to support a growing number of Pans, the real issue was an altered status for untouchables, not how many people get to be fed at a wedding, or whether Liringa would make a better headman than the incumbent, but the redistribution of village wealth or the provision of some source of income for untouchables other than working for their Kond masters—in either case, some kind of Pan emancipation. That would entail a redistribution of the symbols of status and honor. The lockout resolution, if carried through, would have put to the test the basic lie through which Konds buttressed their identity and their self-respect; the outcome might have been disillusion. Their very selves would have been at risk of degradation.

The Konds chose not to let that issue surface onto an agenda, because at some level of awareness they felt that to deal with it openly would be to court disaster.[18] The Pans too may have had fears that their world could fall apart, or perhaps more likely,

[18]If they never spoke of it, how do I know that the fear of revolution was in Kond minds? Both Konds and Pans were aware that times were changing, that Gandhi's influence was on the side of the Pans, that Pans in Bisipara were protesting vigorously and more or less with impunity and that perhaps the time was past when Pans had to be deferential to Konds. The Konds knew that something was going wrong and that there were too many Pans around the place and Pans were getting above themselves. Of course not everyone put all the pieces together to make a neat analytic package, as the schoolmaster did, but that is not the point. One does not need a clear analytic understanding of what a danger is before one has a sense of danger; indeed, the essence of fear is what is present and threatening but not understood.

they were more keenly aware that they had to make a living. In short, both parties tacitly agreed that the "official" version of the distribution of power should stay as it was and not be a present issue. Everyone in Baderi who was aware of the issue, I assume, saw an advantage in *not* using it; the costs, material and emotional, would be too high.

Villagers, whether in Bisipara or Baderi, to some degree operate within a single syntactical system. They share values and beliefs about the nature of their society and about each other, and see themselves as members of the same moral community; obliged to treat one another as moral beings, ends in themselves, rather than as instruments. That this was so in Baderi, even during the troubles, is demonstrated by the implicit claim of the Pans to be treated as *praja* rather than as employees. My third case—the Bisipara cooperative—will show that collusive lying may be found even when there is a marked discontinuity in culture and when the parties clearly consider themselves *not* to be members of the one moral community.

I went back to Bisipara after an absence of four years. This was in the late 1950s, when Harold Macmillan's "wind of change" blew strongly (he made that famous speech in 1960) and optimistic falsehoods about Third World development were more abundant than they later became. After four years I anticipated changes.

Virtually nothing, however, had changed: no paved streets, no electricity, no new wells, even most of the old people still alive. But there had been some "development" in the form of a government-sponsored agricultural cooperative. Its function was to provide improved seed and fertilizer at controlled prices and to grant improvement loans to farmers who had the required collateral—that is, some land. About three-quarters of the households in Bisipara were credit worthy.

On the day I arrived two middle-level officials were conducting an inquiry into the demise of the cooperative. It seems that the secretary, a salaried government-appointed clerk from a village in another region, had absconded not only with the cash in hand (so the villagers said) but also with the records of all transactions conducted since the cooperative had been inaugurated. The records included, of course, the names of those who had taken loans.

I watched a confrontation, with much aggressive posturing by the officials, who were questioning villagers (hectoring and bullying them), individually and in groups, about who owed money. The standard answer was: "Who knows? Someone must owe money. But I never had a loan and I personally do not know anyone who did." At the end of the day the weary senior official confided to me: "These fellows are all liars and rascals. But what to do? We are not police; we cannot hammer them. The money is gone."

The villagers did have a negotiating position that was framed in impeccable logic but also was very cheeky—*chutzpah*, in fact. After all, they told me, the fault was the government's for appointing an outsider as clerk, when there were several young men in the village who could have done the job. Outsiders, the government should have known, are always untrustworthy. But the damage was done; the money was gone. The only sensible course now was to write off the debt, refinance the institution, and open up again, this time with a local lad in charge of the books.

This suggestion was not acceptable to government (if it was ever made),[19] and so far as I know the matter ended there. Nothing was paid back, although several people knew (or claimed to know) what everyone else had borrowed. Nor was the institution reopened. What really happened to the account books (or to the bookkeeper for that matter) I do not know. But I do know the reason why the villagers got away scot-free with the spoils; it has to do both with basic lies and with ordinary lies.

The villagers in Bisipara know that the raj (what they call the

[19]The villagers told me this was their argument, but I did not hear them make it to the officials and I doubt whether they in fact did so; it would hardly have been diplomatic, nor would it have been in accord with the basic lie that framed relationships between villagers and administrators. I will come to that soon.

government when they want it to do something for them) is awesomely powerful and should be nurturant, providing for them like a parent. Thus, at one level, they accept the government's lie about itself. But the villagers also know that the raj reaches these high standards only intermittently because it is staffed by officials who are sometimes lazy and incompetent and often unpredictable. Villagers also know that *all* outsiders, officials and others, are beyond the pale of the villagers' moral community and are therefore dangerous; by the same reasoning, one has the right to deceive and exploit them, given the opportunity to do so with impunity.

Officials, in their turn, know that villagers are uneducated, generally obtuse, overly suspicious, and therefore obstructive, incapable of recognizing their own long-term interests, regrettably parochial in their concerns, and utterly without respect for the truth. A few politicians may be able charm them into cooperation (as Gandhi did); an official, however, has no alternative but to dominate them with the carrot and the stick.

Raj and peasant (at least in areas like Bisipara at that time) constitute a dichotomous structure, but of a peculiar kind. The dichotomy is rooted in differences of culture and a marked lack of crosscutting ties—and, of course, a long history. It is generally agreed that in structures where the two sides see each other as different creatures, and lack any go-between, it is hard for them to work their way toward a shared "truth." First, they have difficulty in communicating because they see the world through different syntactical frames and have different ways of defining truth. Second, they belong to different moral communities and do not feel in the least obliged to refrain from deception. The standard example of such a group is the sect of true-believers: its opposite is the coalition.

Nevertheless in the present case there is a degree of primal consensus and the two parties, villagers and officials, have more in common with coalitions than with warring sects, mutual stereotypes notwithstanding. At least in the context of development, certain features of the raj-peasant relationship modify the dichotomy. First, neither party sees itself as sectlike—true-believers united in aims, values, and interests—but much more in the flexible mode of an enterprise, where people calculate costs and benefits. Occasionally officials get "organizational religion" . (usually when it suits them to do so), but by and large being a civil servant is more a matter of having a job than being a devotee of the organization. Second, the *normative* definition of the relationship in the official lie (and in one version of the villagers' lie) denies any dichotomy of interests. The officials (the raj) should be serving the best interests of the people.

In short, the stereotype each party holds of the other, although certainly an article of faith, is not a primary motivation for hostile action, as in the case of, for example, class conflict or religious antagonism. Pragmatism rules. From the peasant point of view the official is dangerous and often malevolent. But he is not an enemy to be eliminated; he is like an imperfectly domesticated animal that nevertheless has its uses for those quick enough to avoid being gored or trampled. Indeed, to dispense entirely with the raj would be unthinkable.

The lie through which each party constructed its definition of the other is enough to explain the absence of that kind of final accord which marked the wedding speeches or even the quiet conclusion of the Baderi troubles. But there was a conclusion to this affair; the villagers, choosing a bird in the hand (along with a sporting, if rather long chance that the officials might just be bamboozled into refinancing the institution) were the victors. That villagers (humble, uneducated and only a few of them literate, contentious among themselves and committing a flagrant breach of the law of contract) should hold the edge over the almighty Indian bureaucracy requires some explanation.

The officials could have made a real issue of the matter, called it theft or embezzlement, threatened the law, brought along a sub-inspector and a couple of constables and looked the other way while a villager or two got "hammered," or picked out a potential quisling and made it worth his while to betray other villagers. But they did none of this. Perhaps they only wanted to get away

49

from these bothersome people and home before dark. Also, I suspect, they had a mind to the civil service maxim that little troubles should be stifled and not allowed to grow into big troubles. At all costs avoid a reputation for lacking judgment and being overzealous. But these motivations apart, their decision to take no further action must have been encouraged by one important basic lie, revealed in the fact that the actual, although temporary, dominance of the villagers was not allowed to emerge into open discourse.

There is a public and ceremonial consensus between peasants and officials about where power is located, and it is played out every time they interact. Both villagers and officials collude in a symbolic pretense that all power lies with the officials and none with the villagers. Villagers ask for things as a favor and not as a right, even when they are sure it is their right. The official is addressed as *huzoor*, that is, "the presence." Alternatively, he is made familiar as *ma-bap*—mother and father, the protector, the provider, the source of one's well-being. In response, officials are curt, condescending, arrogant, and apparently inflated with a sense of their own effortless superiority. Only rarely (but not on this occasion) did I see a villager shout back, and those who did were promptly removed from "the presence."

Officials, even when they are reduced to seeking a compromise, do not conduct themselves in a conciliatory mode. Bargaining that leads to a compromise requires at least the simulacrum of ad hoc equality. When villagers bargain with each other over a marriage or the settlement of a dispute they sit as equals on the ground. When officials deal with villagers they adopt the posture of an adjudicator rather than a negotiator. They sit on chairs and behind a table, while the villagers stand before them or squat in the dust. Indeed, according to the basic lie of bureaucracy, bargaining cannot take place between peasant and official because the latter is like a judge, the guardian of the law and the keeper of principles, seeking a verdict that sharply separates right from wrong. He is not looking for a division of spoils or costs, which is the end of a successful compromise. This remains the official's posture even when the raj is itself a party to the dispute.

In fact all this is to a large extent a facade. Its falsity is an open secret known to both sides and collusively preserved by both of them. The raj is not all-powerful. No government disposes of enough coercion to govern a country, let alone to reform a society. There must be some degree of consent from the people. This consent is manifested in a collusive disregard for certain known realities, which, if recognized, would upset the basis for cooperative activity. Thus the sequence of episodes in a Kondmals wedding wrote past altercations out of the record. In the Baderi troubles, the status problem created by changing economic conditions was deliberately shelved. In the case of the Bisipara cooperative, even when the villagers had a de facto superiority over the officials, they supported the myth and colluded with the officials by presenting a front of humility.

In such maneuvering there is a complicated interaction between basic lies and ordinary lies. The Bisipara villagers protected themselves (and their spoils) by ordinary lies, which they readily admitted (to me) were lies. But at the same time they sheltered behind the basic lie of their own humbleness, their innocence, and their dependency on a nurturant raj.

Basic lies, after the story of the Bisipara cooperative, seem an altogether more complex matter even than in the Baderi case. There is indeed a dominant lie that people can readily describe (the all-powerful raj). But when one looks at the events, there seems to be not a single lie but a repertoire of separate lies, each one adapted to dealing with particular statuses in particular situations. Consider the "simple" villagers of Bisipara and their self-contradictory repertoire of performances. Villagers are simple folk, relying on the goodwill and guidance of the raj, like children on parents, and doing what they are told. They are humble and respectful. Turn the coin over and something quite different appears. Villagers must look after themselves because officials are outsiders, disposing of enough resources to make contact desirable, with power enough to be dangerous, but in the end weak enough to be manipulated and exploited. For obvious reasons the first version is for use in open discourse; the second is open only among the villagers themselves, and in the presence of officials this lie (which is of course perfectly well known to officials) becomes an open secret, to which neither party refers but which both are ready to put to covert use when it is to their advantage.

All three examples of collusive lying occurred in relatively stable situations, in which the strategy of keeping open secrets out of the public domain was agreed. There is a primal consensus about not disturbing the rules governing the way "truth" (a set of basic lies) is to be used. But sometimes these rules themselves come into question and what one side claims to be a primal consensus the other side marks as merely partisan opinion. This can happen in well-regulated arenas, as when marriage negotiations break down; one day the balance of power in Baderi will change enough to make people acknowledge the change; some day perhaps, representatives of the raj will no longer qualify as "the presence." On these occasions something quite simple happens: what had been a basic lie collusively accepted as true is now branded as ordinary falsehood. It can also happen that a proffered primal consensus is disputed from the outset. We will now consider how challenges are made and what is their significance.

Contesting Basic Lies

The outcome of a challenge against someone's definition of the situation depends upon three variables: the existing level of primal consensus, the resources that each party can deploy to make its definition prevail, and the openness with which the confrontation is made.

Other things being equal, the more open the challenge, the less easily is it ignored, the lower the chance of a negotiated settlement, and the greater the likelihood of outright conflict. A challenge delivered in public has about it a Rubicon or "game of chicken" quality: there is no going back. As is well known, this is a potent form of combative behavior.[20] But as the Baderi case showed, if the primal consensus is high, a settlement will be reached, a high level of publicity notwithstanding.

If the challenge is discreet, it may encode and so appeal to some existing level of primal consensus, thus increasing the possibility of a compromise. Alternatively, being discreet and therefore not widely heard, the challenge may be ignored; then, other things being equal (the relevant variable is power), it should pay the challengers to raise their voices.

The complicated interrelationship among the three variables manifests itself in the case of the coalition government that was formed in Orissa in 1959. The Orissa Legislative Assembly numbered 140 members (MLAs or "Emilies") in 1959.[21] In the 1957 elections the Congress party had won 56 seats, most of them in the coastal plains; the main opposition party, Ganatantra Parishad had 51 seats and dominated the hill areas to the west, a region until 1948 for the most part divided into small principalities.[22] For this reason Ganatantra was stigmatized by its opponents as a "feudal" party. The remaining members were distributed among several socialist parties, some Communists, a party called Jharkhand, and independents.

After the election, six of the seven independents were prevailed upon to cross the floor from the opposition benches and join the Congress. The party was further strengthened by eight defectors from Ganatantra and one from the Communist party. In addi-

---

[20]I have in mind the justly famous analysis in Schelling's "Essay on Bargaining" (1963).

[21]These events are described also in Bailey 1963. A more detailed account appears in Bailey 1959, from which the present version (with some anecdotes that come later) are extracted.

[22]India gained independence in 1947. At that time there were many so-called "princely states" ranging from the gigantic, such as Mysore or Hyderabad, to small landed estates. Some of those in eastern India attempted to set up a union and remain independent of the new central government in Delhi. They were swiftly persuaded to "accede to the Union," and by 1948 not only had all those in Orissa done so, but more than one prince was later to be heard boasting that he "personally was first to accede to the Union."

tion, the government was consistently supported by the votes of five Jharkhand party members, all elected from tribal constituencies in the northern part of Orissa bordering the state of Bihar.[23] Despite the floor crossing and the help of their Jharkhand allies, the government had an uncertain voting majority, but it was strengthened because the opposition, combining the far right and the far left, was usually divided.

Parliamentary procedures are built around the two stages of confrontation and encounter. The process of subversion[24] (recruiting supporters from the opponent's ranks) is emasculated in normal times by party discipline (except when "the whip is off" and there is a free vote). In essence parliamentary debates are devices that serve less to find truth in a particular issue than to test party strength. A motion to put the matter to a vote constitutes a confrontation and the vote, once counted, constitutes an encounter; one side has won and the other has lost. In India, which follows the conventions of the British Parliament, the call for a vote on certain kinds of issues constitutes a direct and formal challenge to the ruling party.[25] If the vote is lost, a government must offer its resignation because the vote has demonstrated that it does not have sufficient support to govern.

But these were not normal times, and subversion was openly practiced to a degree unusual in parliamentary regimes. Floor crossing—shifting one's seat from opposition to government benches or vice versa—is a very dramatic and public event, comparable in some ways to the assault on Liringa or to the wedding performances. Such a move is a dramatized statement of

[23]Jharkhand was a flourishing tribal-based party in Bihar. The members elected to the Orissa house were regarded by most Oriyas as outsiders. They invariably chose to address the assembly in Hindi (they had a constitutional right to do so) rather than in Oriya or in English, and a speech by any of them was usually the occasion for none-too-subtle barracking from Oriya assembly members of all the other parties.

[24]See Bailey 1969:28–30 for a discussion of these three terms.

[25]A defeat in the house on a motion of substance—usually appropriations (financial measures) or, of course, a vote of confidence—calls for the resignation of the government.

allegiance, and its consequences are clear: an acknowledged gain for one side and a loss for the other. Where you sit in the assembly is a matter of public observation and is entirely unambiguous.

How long you will stay there and why you choose to stay there, on the other hand, are matters not of fact but of opinion and of guesswork. There was a great deal of speculation, comments varying in their distribution (public discourse, open secret, and secret) and therefore in their deniability. Everyone who chose to speak about the affair in public deplored the apparent readiness of politicians to change their allegiance in return for a personal reward, sometimes material (the most notorious being the gift of an Austin car—a rare prize at that time), sometimes a minor appointment (for example, a deputy ministership), sometimes a favor for their constituency. But *direct* accusations were rarely made in open discourse (except in the anonymous scandal sheets current at the time) and most of the unsavory details were traded only as open secrets. This caution has something to do with the laws of libel and slander, but not much; the politicians, perhaps because more than a few of them were lawyers, were not in the habit of taking each other to court. Rather, I suspect, they were careful to leave accusations deniable because they accepted a basic lie that characterizes this kind of politics—today's enemies may be needed as tomorrow's friends, and one should think twice before inflicting a lasting wound and so earning oneself a lasting enemy.

Those who made the switch, of course, had appropriate definitions of the situation. There was always the ready-made rationale of the public interest: their allegiance to the government would make it stronger and therefore better able to implement the current five-year plan. Alternatively there was the narrower but still legitimate interest of the constituents. So far as I know the man with the Austin car never mentioned it, but he might (with some effrontery) have claimed it enabled him to serve his constituents better. A less outrageous claim—in that place at that time—would have gone like this: joining a party that the voters of the constituency had just rejected was the best possible move for the constituents themselves, because the government now owed them a favor. In a land where the patron-client link is a major fact of life, such a cover story is not implausible.

Whatever the claims made about motivations, the frequency of defections had very practical consequences. The appropriation bill in April 1958 passed by only two votes. It would not have passed at all had not two Congress members who had left the party some days before, along with three other defectors, returned to the fold. What persuaded the defectors to return I do not know, but in order to readmit them a cover story was needed to render the earlier confrontation void. One of them came up with a dramatic tale about having been drugged with whisky; thus stupefied (not being a drinking man), he had been tricked into resigning against his better (sober) judgment. I have no note about what the other one said, but whatever it was, they were welcomed back. They were, so to speak, allowed to pick up their bets when they realized that the hand dealt them was not as good as it first looked.

Then things really began to fall apart for the Congress. By the early spring of 1959 opposition votes numbered 68, and the government vote (including the 5 Jharkhand members but excluding the Speaker, who does not vote) was 71.

On March 16 a man went on hunger strike, sitting under an awning outside the assembly building.[26] The issue concerned the treatment of villagers displaced by the new German-sponsored steel plant being built at Rourkhella, near rich deposits of iron ore in the northeastern part of Orissa. On several occasion the opposition put adjournment motions so that the troubles at Rourkhella could be debated, but these the Speaker disallowed.

[26]This was a common form of extraparliamentary protest and one that was hallowed by its association with Gandhi. Many of the Freedom Fighters who now were part of the Congress government or of the left-wing opposition group had themselves used this method to protest British rule. The possibility that the protester might starve himself to death puts the strongest of moral pressures on those against whom the protest is directed. The protest is, of course, nonviolent, at least in a technical Gandhian sense.

On March 17 they walked out in protest. Nothing happened, and the confrontation was in effect ignored. They walked out again on March 19, and this time they were accompanied by two of the Jharkhand members, whose constituencies were in the Rourk-hella area. The confrontation was at once acknowledged and became an encounter: the government climbed down. That same afternoon it was announced that demolitions at the plant site would be stopped until after an impartial inquiry had been held, the opposition being invited to send a representative to the inquiry. There is no mystery in this swift response. To lose even two more votes would probably have put the Congress government out of office.[27]

At the beginning of April 1959 the government, responding to a question in the assembly, announced that Orissa's second medical college would be located in Sambalpur district in western Orissa. There had been an agitation by Congress members from Ganjam district to have the college built there. When the announcement was made, five of those who represented constituencies in Ganjam resigned the Congress whip and proclaimed themselves independents. The following day three of them withdrew their resignations and applied for readmission. They were allowed to return. Two others, who had taken the lead in the whole affair, stayed out, presumably in the hope that the government, realizing that the loss of these two votes could bring it down, would be willing to negotiate some kind of compromise. Their defection had left the government side of the assembly with a margin of just one vote: 69 to 68 in a house of 140 (two seats were vacant, and remember that the Speaker does not vote).

On May 15 the Congress ministry resigned; on May 22 a three-man coalition ministry was formed, headed by the former

[27]The force that moved the government was not only the high level of publicity of the protest but also its style. The hunger strike was exactly right for the occasion and the place. The assassination of an official, while it would certainly have attracted much publicity, might have been less effective. A challenge delivered in an idiom that is generally considered inappropriate or immoral is more easily rejected than one made, so to speak, within the rules.

Congress chief minister and containing the leader of the Gana-tantra Parishad and one senior Congress MLA. The coalition thus commanded about 110 out of 140 votes, a comfortable and secure majority.

The two Ganjam defectors from the Congress were promptly expelled from the party, retaining their seats as independents.

Those are the events. Now let us look at some of the constructions put upon them.

Several times, in the last strenuous months of political maneuvering, the Congress chief minister had appealed to the opposition to "put the implementation of the plan above party interests." So much time and energy went into maintaining parliamentary support or encouraging parliamentary defections that the proper business of government—to implement the five-year plan[28] and so bring prosperity to all—was being neglected. After the coalition was formed, both he and the Ganatantra leader stated that the way was now clear to take care of the general interest and to put an end to undue pressures exerted by narrow sectional interests.

There were some other comments. The Praja Socialist leader said:

The only motive behind this unusual coalition in Orissa is to share power together. It is wrong to think that it has any other significance at all. But I feel that after this coalition the opposition in Orissa will emerge as a force with definite principles and objectives.

A leading figure in the Ganatantra, speaking immediately after the swearing-in of the new ministry, had a different comment.

It will be quite a great relief to the people of Orissa that the Congress regime has come to an end. [He had come] to-day to witness the liquidation of the Congress party.

[28]Economic and social development is centrally directed in India. By that time the nation was into its second five-year plan.

The Congress chief minister, two weeks before the coalition with his former opponents was announced, had this to say:

As far as I can judge the Orissa Congress will be strengthened and its influence extended to all parts of Orissa, if it accepts the offer of the Ganatantra Parishad to work the Congress policy and programme, [but if it refused the offer, then at the next general election the Congress party] is likely to be entirely crushed.

The divergences are easily described. The parties in the coalition justified it in public as a noble sacrifice of power on their part so that the general interest could better be served both by "implementing the plan" and by curtailing disruptive and selfish politicking. Before the somewhat less public audience of party loyalists, the move is justified as a means to retain power (Congress) or to gain power (Ganatantra). Outside the coalition, the basic lie about implementing the plan is rejected as a plain lie: the real motivation was power.

The two main parties had begun to prepare the ground for their version of truth before the coalition was formally announced. Negotiations took place behind closed doors, but *what* was being done was an *open* secret. The matter was generally known not just because politicians in Orissa, like politicians everywhere, had friends in journalism and were happy to "leak." The leaking was in fact a preparatory strategy designed to legitimize what was about to be done. So in addition to rumors printed in the newspapers, one found the chief minister on several occasions in the assembly appealing to the opposition parties to put "the execution of the plan" above party interests. "The leader of the Opposition too was not taken aback by the appeal," the *Amrita Bazar Patrika* reported. "He made a suitable reply."

I know nothing about the secret negotiations conducted at the time, but it would be inconceivable if they did not include some hard bargaining. There must have been, as the newspapers happily speculated, arguments and confrontations about how the new government was to be constituted, how large the cabinet would be, who was to be a cabinet member and who was to hold what ministry, and so forth. All this was done quietly and although there was much gossip and speculation nothing came out into open discourse (other than much pious talk about party interests taking second place to "implementing the plan") until the coalition was formally announced. In short, something resembling the procedures that shaped the model wedding were also used to create the coalition. Altercations were not admitted to the public record.

There are, however, clear differences between the wedding and what happened in the coalition. In the latter, the primal consensus that brought two of the parties together was not everyone's consensus. When entered into open discourse, it turned out to be a renewed confrontation. "The only motive behind this unusual coalition in Orissa," said the Praja Socialist leader, "is to share power together."[29]

The Congress and the Ganatantra went public with the coalition in a most patent and ceremonial fashion. They did so in order to ratify their agreement, binding each other by formally inviting an audience to the agreement and removing it from the realm of open secrets. Ratification imposes on the settlement the kind of fixity that is characteristic of each succeeding stage in the marriage negotiations: an agreement that neither side will go back on what has been settled, behavior analogous in function to the handshake that "seals" a bargain.

Presentation to an audience in the case of the model wedding also is an act of ratification. The marriage agreement is "registered" before public opinion through the ceremony described. At the same time whatever dirty linen might remain from the haggling is laundered and comes out generalized and clean in the

[29]His point is this: In India supreme authority in each state is vested in the governor, as the representative of the president of India. If parliamentary government breaks down, there ensues "governor's rule." A failure to maintain law and order is the usual occasion for such intervention, but it may also occur when neither party has a sufficient majority to form an effective government. The governor then rules directly through the bureaucracy, and the politicians are out of a job.

ritualized oratory. The point of the ceremony is to notify public opinion that differences have been resolved and all is now in proper order. The purpose of going public is the same in the case of the coalition: to make sure that public opinion gives its support to what has been done. Obviously "what has been done" has to be presented in a version that is conventionally acceptable to the public and that eliminates from the public record whatever is deemed dangerous or disadvantageous.

Implicit in this procedure is a set of basic lies about secrecy, confidentiality, and power. It has two parts: First, the public interest requires, for reasons of harmony or security or efficiency, that some events and actions be kept secret. That was the position of William Casey and John Poindexter and Oliver North when they kept secret the Irangate operations. Second, when an event or an action is by mutual consent made public (that is, formally announced to an audience wider than hitherto) the intention is to fix or "seal" that event by giving it a form that eliminates from the public record any history of strife and uncertainty. Thus framed, the message claims to be *the* truth, asserting that this particular definition of the situation is *the* correct one. It constitutes a challenge that says in effect that the speaker has the right (or the might) to make everyone agree that his version of the way things are and should be is the only valid one. That was the position of Poindexter and North defending themselves before the Senate committee.

The definition may be known to be inexact or incomplete. Everyone is aware, for example, that marriage negotiations involve a lot of hard talking and wrangling. But if no one chooses to challenge the bland official version conveyed in the ceremonies, the reticence itself makes a statement about power: namely, that power is not *at present* an issue. There may indeed have been a contest in the past, the conventions proclaim, but that contest lies in the past and its details have been written out of history. The contestants are agreed about how power is in fact distributed between them and (whether they like that distribution or not) do not intend to challenge it. That particular distribution, therefore, is sealed, and they are ready to work together toward a common goal.

But the theory also has a reverse side. Insofar as the public does not know everything, its power is diminished. Just as one gains an advantage over an enemy by keeping secrets from her, so also one keeps secrets from the people in order to control them, for fear that greater knowledge might diminish the support they give or even make them obstructive. In doing so one limits their options and so diminishes their power. Until the scandal broke, the Irangate conspirators certainly diminished congressional control over government actions in the United States.

In *covertly* withholding information the politicians in Orissa were making an unannounced assumption about their own authority. When they talked to the people at large about implementing the plan but said nothing about party interests, they were implicitly denying that they were accountable to that particular audience in that particular matter.

If the secret is open, those who are being denied the full story (and know it) may respond in several ways. If they collude *willingly* by pretending that they know nothing or if they say that it is none of their business and such matters are best left to those in charge, then the claim to authority without accountability is granted. Oliver North and his fellows would have been happy with such a verdict. Second, people may *overtly* collude and apparently accept what is going on, but only because they are intimidated. North and the right-wing politicians would not have been discontented with that outcome. That is also the situation in which gossip and rumor are likely to flourish. Third, those shown disrespect may demand the full information or, knowing it, may spread it about and make political use of it, as instanced in the gleeful comments of the Ganatantra leader about the demise of the Congress, or in the all-too-briefly sustained public speculation about how much Reagan and Bush knew of what was going on in the Iran conspiracy.

The Cost of Collusion

There is an air of timelessness about the model wedding. It is a routine that repeats itself again and again, an adaptation certainly to the dynamics of becoming mature, a shift in social formation and a redistribution of personnel, but at the same time it is a repetitive process that in its essence does not change over the years. They have done it before and they will do it again.

That seems to be *one* circumstance in which collusive lying can succeed; the lies have become routinized. People both are willing to control the distribution of information and know how to do so. But more is involved than merely a familiar routine. What makes the collusion possible is that both parties have already agreed that any radical redistribution of power between them is not on the agenda. This proposition holds both for the model wedding and for the villagers of Bisipara when they colluded in the mythology of "the presence." In Baderi the immediate conflict was resolved, stopgap fashion, by a massive self-infliction of myopia, by a willful nominalist pretense that ignoring a problem makes it go away. In other words, collusion in all three instances indicates a fundamentally conservative attitude.

Some problems yield to stopgap solutions and myopia; others do not. When they do not, and nothing is done, the costs can be high. If every conflict settled itself when people turned their backs on the issue, pretending that nothing had happened and picking up life as if it were exactly where it was before the quarrel started (as they did in Baderi), then there would be no point in getting into an argument in the first place, social formations would never change, adaptation would never take place, and in good time everyone would vanish from the evolutionary scene. For certain in the Baderi case there was an agenda of unfinished business, at this time suppressed, which must sooner or later erupt. But in the meantime the villagers solved their problems by the simple device of turning back the clock.

There is a lesson in this. It is customary to rejoice when one can "close the book" on a dispute because the fighting has stopped. To resolve a conflict seems like curing a sick person. So the model wedding, the Baderi fracas, and even the case of Bisipara's defunct cooperative seem to end more agreeably than did the coalition affair, which in fact remained open because the losers still saw it as worth their while to carry on the fight. They were motivated, I am sure, by the desire to get power, but the motivations are of less significance than are the consequences of what they did.

The Baderi resolution stopped the fighting and restored cooperation but did nothing to remove underlying problems. This is not a matter of facing *the* truth. The question rather is *which* "truth" (that is, which basic lie) best enables one to cope with reality. The better design is the constructive one that does not paper over the cracks and does not pretend that nothing is wrong when there manifestly is something wrong.

That, of course, is simply my opinion and I am well aware that such judgments are usually safe to make only with hindsight. Be that as it may, continued altercation after the coalition was formed meant that new solutions were being sought. Minds were still open, and to that extent behavior was rational because founded on a wish to experiment. This—the challenging of basic lies—is Max Weber's world of magic, uncertainty, adaptability, and freedom: the other world—collusive pretense—is like his iron cage.[30]

---

[30]In that phrase Weber was making the point in a more particular context: that of an ideology accompanying the "technical and economic conditions of machine production," which constrain and limit the lives of individuals (1958:181). I think the same is true of any ideology, of all true-believers. "What is decisive," Weber wrote elsewhere, "is the trained relentlessness in viewing the realities of life" (1948:126–27).

3 | Lies to Adversaries

Nobody speaks the truth when there's something they must have.

—Elizabeth Bowen, *The House in Paris*

Lies and Status

Bacon's essay "Of Truth," written seventy years after Machiavelli died, has a distinctly Machiavellian air when he talks about the benefits to be got from deception. The advantages of "hiding" the truth, he wrote, are "to lay asleep opposition and to surprise," to keep open a "fair retreat," and "to better discover the mind of another." The disadvantages are, first, that it is a sign of "fearfulness"; second, that it confuses and drives away people who might otherwise be cooperative; and third, that it may forfeit "one of the most principal instruments for action; which is trust and belief" (1909:19–20). Of course, Bacon hardly needs to add, these disadvantages occur only if the deception is detected and condemned. Machiavelli gives a similar message in *The Prince*: "How laudable it is for a prince to keep good faith and live with integrity, and not with astuteness, every one knows. Still the experience of our times shows those princes to have done great things who have had little regard for good faith, and have been able by astuteness to confuse men's brains, and who have ultimately overcome those who have made loyalty their foundation" (1950:66).

These quotations contain certain assumptions. Public affairs are guided by people of influence, who manipulate each other and ordinary people by controlling information, dispensing lies and other forms of deception as needed. Machiavelli's princes do not owe truth to their subjects; they should "confuse men's brains" and *not* make "loyalty their foundation." Bacon was only slightly less cynical. He invoked trust, but in a backhanded way: do not be caught in a lie because that weakens trust. In all this there is a plain recognition of power, of competition for power, and moreover, of the fact that dominance usually antagonizes at least some of those dominated. Untruths provide weapons for the weak to resist the strong and for the strong to moderate the antagonism that their dominance provokes from the weak.

In this philosophy (certainly in Machiavelli's version of it), political calculations about people run along two unequal dimensions: friend or enemy or neutral; superior or inferior or equal. The dimensions are unequal because the first, solidarity, is subordinate to the second, power. Friendship, for example, is not an end in itself but merely a factor in calculations about power; enmity is significant only because it makes control more difficult. All statuses on the power dimension (including equality) carry with them a right to deceive. The strong use lies (Machiavelli's "fraud") to control the weak, who have no absolute right to know the truth. That seems to be the opinion of Plato, Machiavelli, Francis Bacon, Richard Nixon, Margaret Thatcher, Oliver North, university administrators, and anyone else charged with the management of public affairs. On the other hand, since it is well known that truthfulness is not owed by a potential victim to a thief, if rulers are the thieves of liberty, then they too have no absolute right to truthfulness from subjects. Distinguished defenders of that point of view are not easy to find.[1]

[1]The question in its nonpolitical version—whether truth is owed to a would-be murderer inquiring where the intended victim is hiding or to a burglar

Even less palatable, I suspect, is my third proposition: those who claim to stand above the fray and hold the ring impartially for truth either lie or deceive themselves. Whether they wish it or not, whether they realize it or not, umpires are always drawn into the contest and, if they are to be effective, must, like any other contestant, strive to make their own definition of the situation, their own basic lie, prevail. But as in the case of truth itself, we shrink from the notion that justice, standing impartial above the fray, may be nothing but a necessary illusion and in reality may either be a deceitful claim made by an interested party or a pretense collusively sustained by all parties because they fear uncertainty.

We begin with the view upwards: how the weak use untruth to protect themselves from the strong.

Lying to the Strong

Lying to the strong is a generalized version of the Fifth Amendment: truth could be dangerous because it might give the dominant adversary another weapon. This is not like collusive lying for mutual advantage, a matter of open secrets. The game is played with real secrets and is zero-sum: the power I get from a successful lie is your loss, and your gain is the secret I fail to keep or the deception you uncover.

The game at its simplest has two players, each trying to outwit the other. But often a third party enters the arena: mediator, arbitrator, judge, public opinion, or (a different but overlapping set) ethnographer, sociologist, muckraking journalist, and, slightly more removed, historian. All these persons are supposedly searchers for truth. They enter my inquiry precisely because they claim to have found an Archimedean "place to stand"

---

demanding to be told where your money is hidden—has been asked and answered many times. See Bok 1979:41–44.

and to have access to an objective truth, which I believe is, *in the practice of politics*, unattainable.

I begin with the ethnographer and the informant, an exemplary political interaction (albeit considered a failure if the two merely use each other and do not pretend to at least a simulacrum of disinterested friendship). For sure, there is some ambiguity and much pretense, but in fact power, and hence deception, are present in every strand of the relationship.

"Deception, misinterpretation, misinformation and self-deception are intrinsic properties of any investigator-informant relationship," wrote Myrdene Anderson (1986:323). There are many wry stories about ethnographers bamboozled by the people they call "informants."[2] The informant may fabricate wild fantasies to please the ethnographer or just for his own amusement. "Look!" says one native to another, as they watch their friend talking earnestly to the white man in the solar topee and shorts that resemble a divided skirt, "He's telling that tale about ancestors coming out of a hole in the ground. I don't know how he keeps his face straight!" When not fantasizing, natives may be plainly uncooperative or downright rude (by the ethnographer's standards, of course, but perhaps not by their own), as sundry Nuer were to Evans-Pritchard (1940:10–13). When not being directly obstructive and uncommunicative, they may deliberately sow confusion. Today's verities are contradicted tomorrow. One man's version of the genealogy is significantly different from his cousin's, as I discovered in Baderi.

The habit of protective concealment, an "economical" use of the truth which is the precursor of more direct forms of deception, is ubiquitous, and there is nothing uncommon about it or about the accompanying itch to penetrate the privacy of others. Meeting someone on a path around Bisipara, the standard greet-

---

[2]"Informant" is supposed to be a neutral and less patronizing equivalent for "native," but being unfortunately close to "informer," it can have, as we will see, sinister connotations.

ing is "Where are you going?" or "Where have you been?" and the polite answer is "Out walking!" or "Who knows?" If that last reply seems a little strange, think how people in California respond to "How are you today?" The correct answer, even if you are moribund, is "Just fine!" Privacy is a must, even in suffering. A sure way to disconcert inquirers is to tell them how in fact you are; "I am having this trouble with my lower back . . ."

The ethnographer has a problem: how to intrude on the native's privacy. There are many stories (apocryphal, one hopes), funny in the telling but morally disturbing in their implications. They all concern the exercise of power, in subtle or in unsubtle ways. One of our great elders surveyed native cultures from the deck of a river gunboat. When the boat came to a village, a detachment of soldiers leaped ashore in pursuit of the fleeing natives. They captured mostly old people who could not run fast, but that was all for the best, because the old have a better knowledge of native lore than do the young.

Another way was to pay the native. About the time I first went to India (early 1950s) there was a lot of gratuitous advice to be picked up about the morality and the expediency of paying informants. One might with propriety *hire* an *assistant* (for example, to record or translate texts) and pay him or her a wage, but the genuine *informant* received *gifts*. This distinction removed the relationship (at least in rhetoric) from the marketplace and put it on the moral basis of a prestation.[3] That, I suppose, was the reason for the otherwise quite illogical assumption that information bought must be less reliable than information given. Sometimes marketplace attitudes broke through, as when an Indian colleague, hugging himself, told me that he paid a Toda priest for reciting a particular prayer a fraction of what the old

---

[3]*Prestation* is a French word meaning the dues that are owed by virtue of a particular status. The word has been anglicized. It refers to exchanges of goods or services which symbolize the nature of a relationship; for example, wedding gifts, birthday presents, an engagement ring, and a salute are primarily status markers (or claims). Prestations are contrasted with exchanges that are mainly or only of economic significance. See Mauss 1966.

man had extracted from a distinguished but unwary European ethnographer for the same prayer. The transcription of another Toda recitation is said to have in the middle of it this sentence: "Five more rupees, or I stop right here!" Prayers and spells and ritual procedures that are arcana in the native culture, seem particularly to anesthetize ethnographic scruples. Some informants—we are still in the land of hearsay—were enticed away from the tribal territory, transported to the nearest fleshpot, plied with drink, and thus persuaded to yield up the secrets entrusted to their care.

Those, one hopes, were exceptional cases. Few of us went further than "gifts to informants." We handed out medicines, interceded with authorities, and in general sought a role that would allow us, despite being outsiders, to appear well-disposed. It could happen by accident. A colleague, working in central Africa at the time of the proposed federation, when hostility toward whites was particularly acute, unwittingly endeared himself to the natives by staying away from the local celebrations for Queen Elizabeth's coronation. He thought the monarchy nonsense anyway and saw nothing to celebrate.

Most anthropologists claim friends among the native population, and some have written warmly about these relationships. In rare cases there have been marriages. Nevertheless, ethnography, like journalism or any kind of writing about nonimagined people, including the not-too-distant dead, can rarely be done without intrusion, without the exercise of power or trickery. It requires a foot in the door and a skin thick enough to face down another's reluctance. The victim naturally protects her privacy by silence or by subterfuge; feigned ignorance, outright lies, and tours conducted up a garden path.

One way to get a foot in the door is to question people about other people and that, willy-nilly, gets into gossip. Even when inquiries are direct—"Are you a virgin?" "Do you use condoms?" "How near are you to being an alcoholic?" "Would you vote for Mrs Thatcher again?"—any answer could have obvious social consequences if it reached the informant's friends or enemies. Anyone investigating a community, whether traditional anthropological targets (a village or a tribe) or modern institutions (universities or prisons or hospitals), inevitably gets involved with a network of people in which the informant also is entangled. Imagine the stranger-anthropologist establishing an apparently warm relationship with someone you know has scant affection for you. Would you not worry about your reputation? Would you not be tempted to get in with your own tales first or perhaps spread a little malicious gossip about the informant's treachery? In all directions reputations are put at risk (Wilson 1974).

> Who steals my purse steals trash; 'tis something, nothing;
> 'Twas mine, 'Tis his, and has been slave to thousands;
> But he that filches from me my good name
> Robs me of that which not enriches him,
> And makes me poor indeed.

The hypocritical Iago again, perpetrator of the wicked lie, and mistaken also, for in the competitive world of reputations my impoverishment can be your enrichment. A good reputation is social capital, credits that can be cashed to influence people. A good reputation is power.

Reputations are important in part because the contestants in the arena do not stand alone: they stand before an audience. Malicious gossip, true or false, is dangerous not immediately from the malice of the gossiper but from an authority that is reputedly harsh and unforgiving: public opinion.

Public opinion is not easily avoided. If you are without ambition and try to opt out of the game and be neither a talker nor a listener, the penalty is to be considered what French villagers call *sauvage*: animallike, undomesticated, not part of the community (See Blaxter 1971). The saintly solution, recommended by Gandhi, Lord Baden-Powell, Adlai Stevenson, and Richard Nixon,[4] is

---

[4]My authority for this unlikely inclusion is Nixon himself (*ipse dixit*) in a television interview in 1982: "Don't try to phoney it up!" Of course he may only have been echoing Francis Bacon or Hitler: If you have to tell a lie, make it a good one.

to speak out but speak only the truth. That should cause some social bruising and in any case is really no solution, because truth does not identify itself. *Other people* make the decision. Your good reputation, as Bacon and Machiavelli and many others noticed, depends not on speaking the truth but on people's believing you are speaking the truth (especially when you are not).

A solution, sometimes risky, is to gossip: spread information but take no responsibility. The danger once again comes from public opinion and derives from a basic lie about the nature of communities: that communities are harmonious and the good citizen never gets into a fight. To be seen attacking someone's reputation is, other things being equal, to be a mischief-maker. Since one can never be sure whether other things are equal, it is prudent to disguise antagonism and make one's attack without being seen to do so, to gossip and start a rumor or choose words that have the force of an accusation but the form of innocent comment or even commendation. "How courageous!" you say, when all but the most naïve will understand you mean "How very stupid!"

In short, when informants set up roadblocks or diversions for the innocent ethnographer, they likely see themselves protecting their own reputations, thwarting their enemies, and preserving the fabric of social order from damage by intrusive investigation. A similar rhetoric is available to justify control of information (secrecy and deception) within their own communities. Deception, at least in the mild form of withholding information, is a social and political necessity.

This pattern holds no less strongly for the ethnographer. Anthropology, like government, has usually been practiced downwards, the investigator coming from a social stratum superior to that of the native in power and resources. There have been exceptions. A few bold ethnographers have ventured into *yaghestan,* the land of freedom (or disorder, if you prefer to see it that way). Sometimes, even where the government's writ runs, the natives have a temporary upper hand, as in the case of the Bisipara cooperative. But the usual experience is research in a society, whether colonial or postcolonial or metropolitan, where the natives can reasonably assume that the ethnographer has a more natural affinity with their rulers than with themselves. The fieldworker then must disconnect himself from the authorities to earn trust from the natives, and at the same time keep connections with the authorities so that they will not throw him out and will listen to him when he has something to say to them about "his" people.[5]

That sentence should make it clear that field research requires some skill at deception. One might suppose that detachment, the knack of sitting comfortably on a fence, not leaning too much in either direction but keeping a nice balance, would also be useful. But in fact that kind of cool neutrality is rarely, if ever, achieved. In all cases known to me the ethnographer became a partisan for his or her people and more or less an object of mistrust for their rulers.[6] These decisions about where one's sympathies should lie were usually personal (not institutionally enjoined) and often motivated by political convictions. (I am thinking of anthropologists who worked in colonial Africa, particularly in the areas of white settlement.) I suspect also, that at a deeper level, the decision to join one side or the other is part of that universal longing for certainty which is exemplified in the desire for "truth." Sustained fence sitting is hard on the psyche.

The posture of the anthropologist as the natives' ally, ostensibly nonpolitical and nonideological, had been around in Britain since the turn of the century: colonial government, it was claimed, would be more enlightened if administration sought the advice of

---

[5]What authority he has to speak for "his" people and what the very act of translation signifies, will be further considered in Chapter 4.

[6]Essays on two directors of the Rhodes-Livingstone Institute, Godfrey Wilson and Max Gluckman (Brown 1973 and 1979), are salutary reminders of the real obstructiveness that this partisanship provoked from many colonial officials. See also the chapter by James (1973) on Malinowski. It is a pleasant irony that the two best-informed essayists in a book edited by Asad (1973) effectively negate the patronizing assumption of some of the more true-believing contributors: that anthropologists were the simple servants of colonialism.

anthropologists. The obligation in the field was more direct.[7] Few anthropologists hesitated to conceal from local authorities—and omit from subsequent publications—information that might bring trouble down on their informants.

These are recollections of the years following the Second World War, the era of "new nations" and the "wind of change" in Africa, the ending of overt colonialism and of the myth of the "white man's burden." Virtually all these territories are now independent nations. In other words, the basic lie that sustains government has changed. Has that lessened the need for deception?

Since colonial governments are flawed from the outset with a "necessary immorality," then of course their subjects must lie to protect themselves. One might then think, naïvely, that in a free country there is no need to look over one's shoulder to see who might be listening. But that hopeful thought is punctured by the sharply tyrannical regimes that can be found in the Third World. More than that: merely to substitute one basic lie for another does not do away with the need for ordinary lies. Governments are governments everywhere, and nowhere is the watchful eye of "Big Brother" entirely closed—not in Britain, not in France, not in America, nowhere. Big Brother is ubiquitously (if unevenly) menacing. Independence has not brought India the universal altruism that was Gandhi's version of truth. For sure, power has shifted from the bureaucracy to the politicians (to a degree), and some elite groups have declined while others have advanced, and the basic lie that justifies India's social formation is different now from what it was before 1947. But these changes have not made it any less necessary for people to guard themselves by controlling the flow of information. Simulation and dissimulation are still a

---

[7]Action in the field sometimes called for practical sophistry, and "enlightenment" could include destroying information. When the authorities, not understanding the rules of feuding, were intent upon executing a couple of natives, the anthropologist (so he told me) broke into the judge's office and destroyed the records. "No evidence! Couldn't hang 'em! Had to let 'em go!" followed by a chuckle of satisfied recollection.

necessity; only some of the targets (those who are to be deceived) are different.

The Illusion of Justice

The idea that you constantly give off information that enemies manipulate to damage your reputation implies a tension (an unstable balance) between individual and social interests, between self and society. A logical case for their mutual dependency can be made—neither can be defined without invoking the other—and it constitutes a rational basis for altruism and justice (White 1984:76). But there is also a commonsense view that the two sets of interests—individual and social—are complementary only in the sense that they feed off each other and are mutually predatory. Nowhere is the latter view clearer than in the ideas, just outlined, about governments and their subjects.

Society as public opinion, a collection of censorious peers sitting in judgment, is one thing and bad enough; much worse is society as government, an authority self-consciously ruling, arrogating to itself the right to determine what is in the public interest, and powerful enough to enforce its decisions. Governments are widely considered to be without moral self-restraint. "Unlimited power tends to corrupt the minds of those who possess it," said the Earl of Chatham.[8] And Polanyi writes: "We may still doubt, therefore, whether the rulers of any society, however freely self-governed, will ever observe the claims of morality beyond what is needed in order to delude their subjects (and their allies abroad) to trust their professions of morality." (Polanyi 1958:227).

But as always, assertions never stand unchallenged: every proposition exists in tension with its denial. The major denial, of

[8]Anticipating by more than a century Lord Acton's pithier "Power tends to corrupt and absolute power corrupts absolutely."

course, comes from the strong themselves, affirming their own indispensability and their own benevolence. But there are also admissions by the weak that they do indeed require the strong to protect them from others like themselves. This is Leviathan and the danger of a "war of all against all"; it is also those many citizens who write to the *Los Angeles Times* saying they paid their taxes and they want more police on the streets. Predation, then, is a notion in constant tension with justice, which in this context means the preservation of morality—of truth and justice—by authorities.

If subjects believe that rulers are of necessity without morality because rulers are always self-interested, how can they also believe that authorities are the champions of justice? There is, of course, a logical argument demonstrating that self-interest, which motivates predation, cannot exist outside a framework of justice. White states it briefly: "It is ... irrational ... to talk about self-interest or expediency without regard to justice [because] a doctrine of self-interest requires a language in which the self and its interests can be defined, and this language, like all language, will be social in its origin and in its terms. . . . to speak that way is to lose the capacity to form a community with others or to claim a consistent character for oneself; indeed, it is to lose the power of practical reason" (White 1984:76). I doubt whether the practical reasoning of any common person runs along those lines, which, correct though they may be,[9] seem far from a practical world, where freeloading usually pays off, even though logically indefensible and, if generalized, in practice self-defeating.

In folk belief the mediation between self-interest and justice is achieved through persons who are the champions of justice. They often belong to a ruling group (not always—I will consider the others later) but stand apart so that they can intervene on the side

[9]They are correct within a limited framework, for communities of people who are sophisticated in the use of words. But there are beings, primates and ordinary not-philosophically-articulate people, like most of us, who form communities and exhibit altruism in total innocence of White's argument. Behavior exists in more than words. Jim Moore pointed me in this direction.

of justice. This was the posture of anthropologists who claimed to interpret native values to colonial rulers, and it is the position of anyone who stands up to speak for "the people."

Here is a role through which, it is claimed, truth is spoken and justice is introduced into an otherwise immoral government. Champions stand between the weak and the strong, like a bridge for the transmission of a truth that would otherwise have been distorted by status differences. Let us look at a case. It is a story told me by an Indian official, the collector (that is, chief administrator) of a district that before 1947 (when India won independence) was a small kingdom. I will tell the tale, somewhat shortened, as if in his own words.[10]

The former raja (king) was killed in a police firing in the early sixties. His widow (the rani) was still alive and living in the palace when I was there. Essentially it was a battle with the Congress government. The people of the district are tribals, and some of them were killed in that and other firings because they believed that when they were with their raja gunfire could not kill them. On the first few occasions they were right because it happened the police were using tear gas. All that took place before I joined my district.

A man from somewhere up north came to the district and started preaching to the tribals: they should give up meat and liquor. He presented himself as a sort of saint and put about the rumor that he was really the old raja born again. He gained an enormous influence, which he placed at the disposal of the Congress, and indeed their man made quite a respectable showing in a constituency where they had never even dared field a candidate against the rani's nominee.

That didn't bother me, but I got very worried about what he was doing to the tribals. They were having a real "last supper," killing off chickens and goats. Traders and moneylenders and drink sellers started a rumor that these creatures were about to turn into serpents; so the tribals sold them off at distress prices.

---

[10]The collector's story also appears in Bailey 1986, where it has a somewhat different significance.

77

My propaganda against him got nowhere; so eventually I bit on the bullet and externed[11] him from the district, giving him some friendly advice to go on a pilgrimage or something like that.

But there was an election coming along, and I got a lot of pressure from the chief minister to rescind the order so that the saint could use his influence for the Congress. The Dassera festival was coming up, an occasion when rajas traditionally held their durbars,[12] and the saint had announced that he would return and hold his. I pointed out to the chief minister that there could be disorder and possibly firing if the rival parties clashed. The chief minister said, "What is a little firing?" I said law and order were my responsibility, and I refused to yield. I kept him out. But of course I got transferred, and after that the saint returned and the Congress actually won their election.

But things did not turn out too badly. The saint's influence soon waned when the people came to their senses. Also the politicians were just using him. The chief minister had said to me, "After the election you can do what you like. Drown him if you want!"

Clearly, if this is history, it is history seen through the eyes of a man who has an ax to grind in the telling. He has provided a text, a political drama with a moral. There are four actors. At the bottom are the tribals, weak, gullible, innocent, superstitious, much in need of a champion's protection. They have two exploiters. One is the saint (in other words, a Gandhian social worker), an ambiguous figure who is a proselytizer both for Congress and for Hinduism. The other is a politician, the villainous chief minister, whose lack of scruple is vividly conveyed: "What is a little firing?" and "Drown him if you want!" Fourth comes the collector himself, the champion of justice and truth, the hero of his own story.

This tale was told to me in the late seventies, thirty years after

[11]This is a felicitous Indian inversion of "intern." It was much in use during the Freedom Fight, and its meaning is obvious: to forbid someone entry into a particular area.

[12]This is a reception or levee at which the ruler presents himself to his subjects to receive their homage and listen to their petitions.

India won independence, and it is not without irony. The attitude of the collector, a virtuous official protecting his people against the villainy of the politician and his hangers-on (the saint, the drink sellers, the moneylenders, and the rest), captures exactly the spirit of the officials, both Indian and British, in their struggles with Congress politicians during the Freedom Fight. (At that time the collector would have been a child.) It testifies also, of course, to the ubiquity of tension, if not conflict, between officials and politicians. In this case the politician won and the collector failed to protect his charges from the baleful influence of the saint.

Was the collector a mediator armed with the truth, championing justice and standing between the politicians and the common people? He thought so; I think not. As the tale unfolds, notice how the common people, the tribals, seem to fall away from the center of the arena. By the time the story reaches its climax, the tribals have become little more than an excuse, an occasion for another testing of strength between the main antagonists, the bureaucrat and the politician.

Nor does the contest have much to do with truth; it is about power. The unscrupulous and manipulative chief minister is apparently without moral concern, interested only in power. That, willy-nilly, projects the collector into the arena as a combatant and gives him a license to deceive, and he does. He presents himself as artless, simple, straightforward, undevious, fighting the virtuous fight with no more than the weapon of his own principles and the legitimate authority that his position gives him. But the tale he tells is totally slanted and is indeed an artful piece of rhetoric. It is not the simple narrative that it appears to be. The selection of events and the words used to describe them unmistakably mark out virtuous officials from villainous politicians. It is a basic lie, a tale woven out of error (the guileless tribals), deceit (the politicians and their hangers-on), and truth (himself, of course).

The tribals who appear in his story are a sorry lot. They are childlike, superstitious, out of touch with reality. They believe that when their raja is with them, bullets turn to water. They accept a charlatan as the reincarnation of their raja. They believe that chickens and goats will turn into snakes. They cannot recognize their own best interests and are in need of the protection of a more enlightened person who will act like a parent, for they are indeed childlike.[13] Lest anyone think that such attitudes belong only in colonial and ex-colonial countries with authoritarian civil services, or among aristocrats or a bourgeoisie with fascist leanings, it should be remembered that there has been in Marxism a continued, if often disputed, insistence on superior people, the "vanguard," who would provide progressive leadership for a working class incapable of working for, even of knowing, its own best interests. Lenin, pouring scorn on those who would have the Communists a "mass party" instead of a "party of leaders," wrote this:

> The immediate task that confronts the class-conscious vanguard of the international labour movement, i.e., the Communist parties, groups and trends, is to be able *to lead* the broad masses (now, for the most part, slumbering, apathetic, bound by routine, inert and dormant) to their new position, or, rather, to be able to lead *not only* their own party, but also these masses, in their approach, their transition to the new position. (Lenin 1975:97–98, emphasis in original)

"Inert," "dormant," and "slumbering" are not precisely the adjectives that the collector uses for his tribals, nor did he see himself as agitprop for the tribal masses, but he certainly shared with Lenin the same patronizing vision of the incapacities of hoi polloi, the rabble. Hobbes at least honors ordinary Jack and

[13]Once again there are echoes of the Freedom Fight. For exactly these reasons the British excluded certain tribal areas from constitutional reforms that would have given Congress politicians access. The tribals, they claimed, would be exploited by traders and moneylenders and unscrupulous politicians. The Congress politicians, needless to say, saw the matter differently—as a device designed to exclude the tribals from full citizenship and to deprive the Congress of tribal support.

ordinary Jill with the capacity for energetic self-destruction; when the citizens of his commonwealth become politically "inert," they do so voluntarily, disciplining themselves.

To what extent the tribals in the collector's story share the myth of their own incapacity is not clear. Often the humble acquiesce openly (because it pays them to do so), all the while maintaining a robust counterideology of their own. We saw some of that in the case of the Bisipara cooperative, and we will see more shortly. The real "owners" of the myth of paternalism in the present case, however, are not the tribals but their superiors, who are contesting for the right to protect tribal people and therefore to have power over them. The contest signals apparent divisions within the dominant class, and there are indeed such divisions, as the story clearly indicates. But *without any of the contestants having to say so*, the ruling class is no less clearly united on certain fundamentals, in particular the principle that puts Lenin in the same bracket with the collector. All the protagonists in the dispute—the chief minister, the collector, and the saint—in effect agree on where the boundaries of the political arena are to be drawn, on who is qualified to compete for power and who (such as the tribals) is not. Each has a different agenda for the tribals— indifference, paternalism, pseudopoliticization—and each is capable of changing an agenda to suit the occasion (what the chief minister says in public is not what he says privately to the collector), but all, by their postures and actions, proclaim that tribals were not at that time viable political contenders.

The conclusion is inescapable: this is a basic hegemonic lie. It says, to rulers and ruled alike, that only the elite are fit to govern. The real contestants—collector, saint, and chief minister— collude with one another in limiting the right of entry into the political arena and so, in that respect, maintain the existing social and political order.

What does this say about champions? It says that the champions of the poor and weak in certain circumstances and, I suspect, often unknowingly may support the existing social order. They do so in different ways. Some are troubleshooters, like the collector, with solutions that could alleviate material hardship. Others adjust the people to the system, like the saint filling tribal minds with quasi-religious fantasies and offering only fictive remedies for misery and deprivation. But in the end their actions protect those who dominate. How conscious they are of what they are doing is hard to know. They do not admit to hegemony; they do, however, readily accuse each other of lusting for power. But if *motivations* are in doubt, *consequences* are clear. Champions function for the system like lubricant for a machine, preventing the buildup of excessive friction.

Lies to the Weak

The weak use ordinary lies to protect themselves from their rulers. Machiavelli's Prince also uses ordinary lies to keep his subjects down. But Machiavelli's "fraud" encompasses not only ordinary lies but also basic lies—hegemonic lies—designed to win consent from the governed. Force is then kept in reserve for use when consent fails.

Consent from subjects appears in *Leviathan* as enlightened self-interest: if people did not yield sovereignty to the ruler, life would be "solitary, poor, nasty, brutish and short." Hobbes has little to say about truth and deceit in governments and he mostly sails above the question, but his position is clear. Truth is attained through reason and the scriptures. God's truth (scripture) stands independently, an absolute truth. But the truth reached through reason is of a different kind (what now would be called pragmatic). Reason insists that it is in everyone's interest to form "that great sovereign LEVIATHAN called a COMMONWEALTH" (1946:5) and hand over absolute power to a ruler (to "covenant") so that he may prevent people from slaughtering each other. It would be irrational to set limits on the ruler, for that would lead to the destruction of the commonwealth (1946:chap. 18). The subjects, therefore, have no ground on which to question the decisions or the judgment of the ruler, for reason dictates that they must be treated as the truth.

Leviathan is an expression of the perils of the human condition and at the same time a plan for delivering humankind from sufferings brought on themselves by their own essentially selfish nature. It can also be read as a basic lie, a definition of the human situation that tells people why they must have a government and how they should act toward that government. The message to the common person is very clear and very simple, the same message as in Plato's *Republic*: the citizen must do what the state commands.

Ideologies of dominance (I mean ideologies promoted by the rulers, not necessarily those accepted by the majority) justify the exclusion of ordinary people from power in two ways: people are either inert or self-destructive. Both myths are in use, the first when affairs are going smoothly for the rulers and the second when the common people kick over the traces. The distinction has consequences: the ignorant and helpless are like children, to be helped and (within limits) to be educated; but the refractory are to be punished (for everyone's good, including their own, of course).

The myths, including the myth of *noblesse oblige* (that privilege entails responsibility), are charters for repressive regulation. The statement of incompetence presents a moral and political judgment as if it were a technical matter. Positions of privilege are deemed to require command of an esoteric language or some other restricted knowledge that is available only to those few who inherit the right to receive the requisite training or can afford to purchase it. Sometimes, of course, the qualification is genuinely technical; the patient will die under the untrained surgeon's knife or the unqualified engineer's bridge will collapse. But in many cases the training is ritual rather than technical, its only function being to restrict entry to positions of power. In other words, the doctrine of the common person's incompetence is a symbolic expression by dominant people of their own effortless superiority, reinforced by restrictive actions taken in the name of efficiency but having the force of repression. The ideology and its accompanying regulations together keep out the unwashed.

There is an ample repertoire of justification. Appeals to common sense, to greed, to fear, to altruism—all have a part to play. Nor is the deception always straightforward; sometimes its complexion is altered by a filter, as Bok puts it, self-deception serving to keep up the morale or ease the consciences of the rulers. It may also be a collusive pretence by both the weak and their rulers. There are also likely to be complications in the form of apparent antagonisms within the ruling class, as in the case of the collector and his antagonists. Champions like the collector, I concluded, function as a safety valve, a precaution against the system's destroying itself.

Certain popular institutions work the same way. They appear to stand for justice, defying unjust authorities; but in fact they help to keep the rulers in power. Although seeming otherwise, these institutions are thus domesticated within the hegemonic lie that the strong use to gain consent from the weak.

In peasant communities in Europe there were once—and in a few places still are—bands of young men licensed by custom to behave irresponsibly and disruptively, as if in a yearlong carnival. They were in some ways like members of modern urban street gangs (for example, much concerned with territoriality), but they were not, either in their own communities or by the verdict of historians, judged to be criminals. Here is Euclide Milano, writing about Piedmont, once a kingdom, now a part of northern Italy:

These *Companies* or *Societies of Fools*, also called the *Madmen*, or the *Donkeys* or the *Stupids* emerged in Piedmont as a reflection of those festivals of the *Fous* or the *Innocent* which were celebrated in nearby France with a strange mixture of sacred and profane. These were genuine expressions of the spirit of association that belonged to the middle ages, a relic of pagan traditions, and an instrument of rebellion on the part of the bourgeois against the feudal classes and an expression of the idea of liberty against theocratic and reactionary principles. More than anything else they were satires and parodies of feudal and ecclesiastical organization. Their chiefs were given titles such as "abbot" and they called themselves "monks," but they were not in the least dressed like monks and they carried halberds. They demanded official recognition as the holders of special privileges and rights, such as, for example, that of organizing religious and civil festivals, levying taxes on baptisms and marriages, in which they interfered whether they were invited or not. (Milano 1925:90; my translation)

Milano adds that even in his day (early 1920s) young people followed the tradition. It was still to be found in the late 1960s in France. Here is an account by Susan Hutson of a village (Valloire) just across the border from Piedmont:

The *jeunes*—boys between leaving school and marriage—have formed a distinctive group in the village for as long as anyone remembers. The *jeunes* group is primarily an informal leisure group. Every evening members meet in one of the bars—the one with the most doubtful reputation, the most frequented by passing outsiders and the juke box. At weekends, they often drive around in their cars looking for diversion. They descend *en masse* on any local event, attempting to take it over, often by drunken buffoonery. Danger, irresponsibility and clowning are necessary parts of their activities. *Jeunes* organize all traditional public entertainment in the village. For example, the procession at *Mardi Gras* and the summer *fête* were arranged by a *jeunes* committee. They also manage the skiing events—the chief modern village entertainments. (Hutson 1973:36)

These young men, like the Fools in the past, regulate and organize a part of village life which lies outside the family and is not within the domain of government. They mark out a region of their own, where they enjoy autonomy and irresponsibility and where the writ of the household head does not run. At another level their predecessors, the Fools, symbolized peasant auton-

85

omy, that part of peasant life over which the lord had no authority, perhaps because he chose to leave it ungoverned, perhaps also because he did not have the resources to stamp his mark on everything. So, when this autonomy is taken together with the mocking of authority and of the political order, it seems at first sight that the hegemonic lie was being contested and the dominant ideology had met a counterideology. That was Milano's opinion: he perceived "an expression of the idea of liberty against theocratic and reactionary principles."

I doubt it. If that is what they were expressing, they probably did not know it; they were just having fun. If *liberty* means "license" or "letting off steam," then Milano is correct, for without a doubt these are occasions for the release of psychological tension. Mockery, yes; political protest, no. Milano reads in too much that is explicitly ideological.

Moreover, when the Fools were disciplined, it was not for sedition but for extremes of hooliganism. The escapades of the young men in Valloire were tolerated much as the excesses of young men in groups are tolerated elsewhere: drunken parties on the eve of conscription, rugby club dinners, even, until recently, soccer hooligans. The companies of Fools were likewise indulged so long as they stayed within bounds. They were met with the same attitude that carnival encounters: a time of the year or a time of life for letting off steam, healthy and necessary, so long as no severe damage is done to property or to the social order.

Indeed, in one respect the Fools emerge as direct guardians of the social order. Offenders against custom—the widower who marries a maid or, much worse, the older woman marrying a young man—were treated to charivari, a discordant nighttime serenade accompanied by the beating of pots and pans and shouts of derisive obscenity, or to cow muck piled high across the threshold: public opinion at its nastiest. In such small ways the Fools tasted power, while, at the same time, they mocked the power of constituted authorities. When they did step across the limit—Milano writes of rioting and extortion—they were put down: at least for a time.

The young men in the companies of Fools are of the common people. (Aristocrats did it their own way, usually at the expense of the peasants. Manzoni's novel *The Betrothed* has just such a character in Don Rodrigo.) The Fools are not champions of the common people, for a champion is a hero and an individual and they are not; they are collective and faceless. It is this very masked quality (as in carnival) that enables them to mock authority and the social order without being punished. What they do looks like defiance, just as what champions do looks like concern for the deprived; but it is a most equivocal form of defiance. The powerful may be mocked by assuming their titles, but the masters themselves remain untouched. The victims are those among the common people—or close to them—who stand out from the herd: the old man with a young bride, the girl who is jilted, the husband who is henpecked, sometimes the village priest.[14] In short, despite first appearances, the companies of Fools do not give the lie to that basic lie which marks down peasants as natural victims for domination and exploitation by their betters; they are part of that lie and part of that system.

Good Soldier Svejk's creator introduces his novel with a splendidly ironic sentence: "Great times call for great men."[15] There is indeed a heroic quality in those individuals who mock authority and its pretensions, even when they are licensed jesters and still more when, like Svejk, they are unprotected but still dare to beat the system and outwit their masters. Unlike the Fools, the Svejks are not anonymous. They sometimes become folk heroes (or antiheroes, as they are now called). Anyone who has served in the ranks of a large organization, such as an army or a university, has

[14]For what happens to jilted girls and mismatched spouses and sundry other offenders see Milano 1925:102–11. He has a footnote on p. 109 telling how in Saluzzo, if carnival passed without a marriage, it was the custom to put the priest in a wheelbarrow and dump him on a manure pile. He could save himself by paying a fine.

[15]Hasek 1973. The spelling of the hero's name follows Parrott's translation and replaces the more common German form, Schweik, which appeared in an earlier translation.

been treated to recitals of its trickster folklore: the person who, having no authority but fortified with much disrespect, by cunning alone defeats the organization and its owners.

There are also heroes of another kind, for whom the mythology takes a different form. These are outlaws, overt protesters, what E. J. Hobsbawm calls "social bandits" (1959), the best known in the English-speaking world being Robin Hood. The basic lie enshrined in these tales certainly celebrates cunning, but it is the cunning not of the trickster but of the astute leader, the one who knows how to lay a good ambush and who always thinks faster than his opponent. These heroes are usually of humble origin[16] but they invariably have noble qualities, which stand forth to deny what, in the official ideology, characterizes a peasant. In that ideology the peasant is like a domestic animal: cautious, calculating, unimaginative, dour, unromantic, without honor, and chained to work. By contrast the nobleman is a cavalier, adventurous, romantic, impulsive, creative, and above all no weary plodding ploughman.

Robin Hood is a yeoman (in one version of the story) unjustly deprived of his land and so forced to become an outlaw. He robs the rich and gives to the poor. He worships the Virgin but is a foe of monks and abbots and bishops. He outwits the sheriff of Nottingham. He is the protector of women. He is loyal to the true king, Richard, and is a foe of the usurper, John. He lives a life of freedom in Sherwood Forest; his weapon is the weapon of the common soldier, the longbow. His enemies are the enemies of the common people—prelates and law officers and the gentry.

But in other ways he is not like a peasant or a yeoman. He does not cultivate the land; he does not raise a family; he has romantic adventures with noble ladies; he is chivalrous; he is generous and openhanded; he is free, gracious, brave; in short he is like the ideal of a nobleman. At yet another level he stands above even the

---

[16]Certainly this is so in the case of the social bandits; stories about Robin Hood's extraction vary between yeoman and nobleman.

nobles. He is invincible;[17] he can defy agents of the law because he is smarter than they are. Finally, although an outlaw he is the ultimately moral person, friend of the true king, enemy of the usurper, friend of the common people, having just those noble qualities that most noblemen in reality lack.

The companies of Fools, except for those occasions when they genuinely run riot, are part of the established system and help to keep it in being. The message they give is that oppression and domination are not pervasive; the rulers grant space for the common people to run their own lives (to a degree) and to enjoy themselves. Thus, as I have said, the companies of Fools are part of the hegemonic lie: they help the existing system of dominance to survive. The Svejks do not, but neither do they oppose it; indeed, like parasites feeding on a host, they need the system. The message they give is that there is no need for (perhaps also no possibility of) overt resistance, and in any case freedom can be had by evasion and cunning. To that extent they too function as a safety valve.

But Robin Hood is different. If he existed and if his adventures were like those told in the tales, then, albeit a loyal subject of King Richard, he was also in a small way promoting revolution. Kidnapping the rich, holding them to ransom, forcibly redistributing their property are actions directly upon the world. Other bandits in more recent times and down to the present, for example in Sicily and in western and northern India, exist as part of the historical record and had a direct (although usually short-lived) effect on the world around them. The deeds of all such outlaws, whether fantasy or reality, have a wide influence as messages, constituting a definition of the situation that runs counter to ideologies of dominance.

---

[17]Most of the stories I have found about Robin Hood have a "happily ever after" ending. The social bandits nearer our time described in Hobsbawm 1959 invariably are killed, but only after miraculous escapes and always (the myths have it) through betrayal by a trusted person.

I have been writing mostly about peasant societies, but the example of Svejk suggest that mythologies apparently contradicting, or partially contradicting or openly denying, the dominant ideology can be found in other social formations. Some of these mythologies are genuinely revolutionary. Outlaws and social bandits are now called terrorists (or freedom fighters) and are rhetorically more sophisticated than their rural predecessors, skilled in making sure that the message of their violence is broadcast and not left to speak for itself. Other forms of protest fall into the category of the safety valve that protects the system from its own excessive states. The little man as trickster is found everywhere and is the more admired as formal organizations become larger, more impersonal, more pompous, more rigid, and therefore more ripe for ridicule. But the little man is at best an irritant, not a destroyer, not a revolutionary.

Let us look finally at one very contemporary institution of seeming protest; what journalists call "investigative reporting" and its victims call "muckraking." It has some very distant affinities with charivari and the like, penalizing offenders against the social order. It also has affinities with social control through gossip or the spreading of scandal, except that in these cases an author takes responsibility (of a sort) for what he or she puts out.

Investigative reporting of public figures is not new: no one learns the classical languages without learning also about the wickedness of Cataline or the corrupting influence of Socrates. In the eighteenth century readers of the London *Public Advertiser* were treated to the "Letters of Junius," a sustained attack on the morals and capacities of various public figures, including King George III. But in the modern age muckraking has emerged both as a literary[18] form and a political weapon. Immensely improved

[18]The adjective is perhaps somewhat generous. The style is neodictaphonese, short-winded, designed for those whose attention span can cope with sentences of no more than twelve words and paragrahs of no more than two sentences. A good example is Bob Woodward's (1987) *Veil: The Secret Wars of the CIA, 1981–1987.*

techniques of mass communication make it both possible and profitable. Daniel Boorstin's "explosion" of image making (1963) has clearly led to an explosion in image wrecking.

At first sight this seems to be an activity that runs absolutely counter to the dominant ideology, for its purpose is to show how the rich and the powerful, whose position is validated in the myth of dominance, are not what they claim to be but are liars or cheats or fornicators. As I write, the fractured sewer of Irangate still occasionally fertilizes the news media. Recently several prominent financiers were exposed as criminals, and—a joy to fans of the political game in America—two well-known television preachers, one caught in fornication and the other in certain more ingenious lecheries, fell symbolically on each others' swords.

Should investigative journalists be seen as a kind of nonviolent dissident, heroically protesting the dominant ideology? The answer is clear once one realizes that the victim is always primarily a person or persons and only as an afterthought is blame attached to the system. It is true, of course, that successful investigations will tarnish the entire institution; the television ministries reported a distressing drop in contributions after the Bakker and Swaggart escapades. There are also usually calls for legislation and regulation that will make it more difficult in the future for nonelected officials to make de facto policy decisions or financiers to rig the market. But first and foremost the muck is raked to find sinners and sins, not to identify defects in a system. These are like witchcraft accusations in tribal Africa. When things go wrong it is because people have not lived the pure and moral life, and the remedy is to exact public repentance. Institutions are fine; only people are bad—a verdict no less idiotically incomplete than "Guns don't kill people. People do."

In their effect on the dominant ideology these investigative forays and the companies of Fools are much the same. They provide a simulacrum of criticism and the illusion of an open society and of a governing class responsive to those below it. But in fact the dominant ideology is left intact; it is even fortified by putting the blame on individuals rather than on the social order.

Sometimes the arrows of investigative journalism land on the target and a public figure is impeached or disgraced.[19] When that happens, we may be tempted to agree with the Vulgate and conclude that truth is great and has prevailed. That would be a mistake; what has prevailed is not truth but the basic hegemonic lie. Justice, the lie says, has prevailed and the rulers are honest. As one of them said when the Pentagon scandals of 1988 broke loose, "You have to expect one or two rotten apples in a barrel that big." Apples in a pork barrel? Alternatively we can take the disingenuous word of the gentleman interviewed about an apparently scandalous connection between campaign contributions and judicial decisions in Texas: "Mr. Wallace, I'm not commenting on the question. I'm just reporting the facts. Pigs is pigs!"[20]

He was "just reporting the facts": in other words, he was speaking the truth, not just his opinion but the real truth. Muckraking would not be possible if there were not a clear folk notion that there is objective truth and there is straightforward deceit and dishonesty. The moral forcefulness of "truth" is well shown when selling arms to the wrong people or playing around with ladies of easy virtue (you can excuse yourself with "I did it for my country" or "Everyone does it") turns out not to be the deadlier charge; the real damage is done by being caught in a lie, perjuring oneself before congressional committees or (in the case of the two preachers) being a hypocrite.

There is also a generic defense against muckraking which has the same significance. The victim and the victim's defenders may set out to define the affair as a "media event," a phrase that means it is an event imaginatively created for political purposes, not one that has in it any historical or objective truth. Its goal is not to

---

[19]Not only are many of those caught with their hand in the public purse defiant, but occasionally they are joined in this defiance by their voters. There is a whiff of Svejkism in this: sympathy for the small victim of a giant bureaucratic or legal machine. One corrupt politician, brought to trial, convicted, and awaiting sentence, was nevertheless voted back into the public office that he had used to extort bribes.

[20]*Sixty Minutes*, September 25, 1988.

bring honest standards back to government or to introduce morality into televangelism but to smear an administration or to take over a prosperous ministry or to show that journalists and other commentators have political clout or merely to profit from sensationalism through increased circulation or improved program ratings.

In such situations Pilate might well have asked, "Where is Truth?" and concluded it was nowhere. Words are being used less to find out what happened than to persuade those who matter to accept a particular version of what happened and how it should be understood. Obviously each party has its own particular ax to grind, and who is defined as the victim and who is the target of persuasion will vary with each version of each case. Certainly objectivity is off the stage.

Seasonable Truth

Some of the deeds and words that I have described in this chapter bid fair to qualify for Bok's "clear-cut lie." They are "ordinary" lies, as distinct from "basic" lies. I doubt whether the traders and moneylenders who spread the rumor about the imminent transformation of chickens and goats into snakes believed that was going to happen. The ethnographer's informants, I assume, at least on some occasions "keep open a fair retreat" by deliberately concealing what they know or by telling fairy stories. One of the joys of reading about Svejk's escapades is the sheer effrontery of manipulative lies told under vivid protestations of truth.

How odious they are as lies is harder to judge, because that depends on consequences and guesses about motivation and on what values are used to make the judgment. The informant who deliberately misleads the ethnographer comes out well if you decide he was protecting himself and his society (truth is owed neither to a thief nor to an ethnographer) and badly if you can

93

bring yourself to believe that he irresponsibly deprived a scientist of necessary information. In other words, the wickedness of the informant's lie is relative to the context in which you choose to place it; and you do have a choice. It is still, of course, a lie.

Such an unambiguous designation cannot so easily be made in the case of more ambitious forms of untruth, the basic lies used to buttress positions of power or to foment resistance and revolution against a dominant class. Myths or ideologies are not clear-cut lies, but they are untruths that serve to "lay asleep opposition" or "to confuse men's minds." Depending on your point of view—let us say Hobbes or Plato versus those who write editorials in the *Los Angeles Times*[21]—fraud used to control subjects may be for their own good or always to their detriment. There is, as I have said, an ample vocabulary available to make one or the other judgmental definition of a particular ideology: it may be presented as scripture enshrining eternal verities or it may be branded a collection of barefaced and cynical lies.

It would indeed be a relief to uncover an eternal verity, to be able to say that truth and justice were not, after all, illusions. It is even a small relief to find that all lies are not barefaced insofar as manufacturers of ideologies often manage to deceive themselves. But for the most part, as I have worked through the various examples, it has been clear that whatever adversaries assert to be the truth usually turns out to be what they think is in their own interest (or their mutual interest, if they reach a compromise). Often the way they behave does not accord with what they say about their motivations and intentions. When they claim that their "truth" is an objectively tested truth and *the* truth, the claim is simply fraudulent. There is not one truth: there are many truths, each manufactured within a particular system and to suit particular interests. Adlai Stevenson's admonition to himself and other would-be rulers invites parody: Politicians must "cling

[21]For them true wickedness seems to be any restriction whatsoever on the free circulation of information, no matter how scandalous or disgusting or injurious. But they are not without prudence for themselves, as when they refused to publish a cartoon strip that lampooned Frank Sinatra.

everlastingly" to whatever brand of "truth" will put them in power.

The world is thus becoming alarmingly relativist, everyone, in the end, having his own truth. But to paraphrase Marx on history, men make their own truth, but "they do not make it just as they please; they do not make it under circumstances chosen by themselves, but under circumstances directly encountered, given and transmitted from the past" (1981:15). In the final chapter I will ask what these circumstances might be; where, if anywhere, Archimedes might stand to move the world. Is there, after all, a truth that is not illusory?

4 | Do What You Will?

Do what you will, this world's a fiction
And is made up of contradiction.
                —William Blake

Where to Stand?

Marx, in the sentence quoted at the end of the last chapter, was talking about tradition and the difficulties people have in recognizing the newness of new things; they see the present in the image of the past. "The tradition of all the dead generations weighs like a nightmare on the brain of the living," he wrote, with a touch of Victorian melodrama (1981:15). He goes on more prosaically to explain that just as the beginner at a second language has to think in his mother tongue, so, when a new social formation emerges, people continue to think in the idiom of past formations. But mastery lets one think in the new language and the old language is put aside; social formations, too, in the end find their own interpreters, who create a style of thinking that is purified of the past and its dead generations. Tradition and culture, in other words, are epiphenomena that eventually adjust themselves to an underlying social reality.

Marx does have a place to stand, and so he can move the world. His social reality is assumed to be an objective thing, a reality that explains how societies work and how men behave. It can be uncovered by asking two questions that apply everywhere. What are the means of production? Who controls them? In that way he resolved for himself the problem of objectivity and gave himself a foundation on which to build.

We have a similar problem. If there is no objective world, no rock to stand on, then it may be that there is also no objective way to sort out the weaker from the stronger "truth" and no control on the use of untruths. That would not matter if the different versions had no other purpose than to amuse or delight. If aesthetics failed and we could not decide which version is the prettiest, and for some reason we still wanted a decision, it could be made by spinning a coin or arm wrestling or taking a vote: that way we could pick the best "truth." But truths, at least in politics, are not just for entertainment: they purport to be plans to cope with a real world. They provide a basis for action, and we get the results back in the form of experience.

That is why politicians believe (or say they believe) in the idea of an objective truth, standing opposed to error and deceit. It guides them in what they do. Politicians have minds, they would argue, and politicians think, but politicians are not merely thinkers, contemplating the world; they are also movers and shakers, molding and changing that world. But then they confound us and each other by throwing into the ring so many incompatible versions of truth that it is difficult, perhaps impossible, to know which "truth" is the real truth, or even, failing that, whether one "truth" is any better than another.

If people lived not in societies but in perfect privacy, their idiosyncratic versions of the world would be disturbed only by experiencing the brute facts of nature, being burned by fire or poisoned by oleander or discovering that, unlike the birds, they cannot fly. But since they live in societies, their versions of reality are also constantly being challenged by the versions of other people. Only those privileged by very high status[1] or by incar-

---

[1] I once knew a very distinguished and slightly self-important scientist who pronounced the first syllable of "schizophrenia" in a manner that is best de-

ceration in the madhouse are routinely exempted from taking heed of such challenges.

Thus there is a competitive interchange between upholders of disparate and incompatible world views. From one point of view, this is a process of education. That is how we see it when we come to agree that another person's version is superior to our own. We have learned something. When we accept it, we say that it is "objectively" true; the world is round, after all, because you can sail round it or fly a plane round it and you might as well also agree with Copernicus, despite the evidence of your eyes, that the earth does go round the sun. "Great is truth and it prevails," it is written in the Vulgate, an appropriately commonplace sentiment, and we should be sustained (if we believe it), because it must mean that those who deal in truth will vanquish the deceitful.

But we may also defer to someone else's version, although we believe it to be false, because it pays us to do so. The personal costs of accepting it seem relatively small and the penalties for not agreeing are great: *Eppur si muove*,[2] the story has it Galileo said in frustration, risking his recantation. Galileo recanted because those who wanted him to admit that the sun went round the earth were powerful, thus demonstrating that this traffic in different versions of reality is, at least to some extent, regulated by power. But this is not merely the simple truth that those who have coercive force at their disposal, like Galileo's prosecutors, are in a better position to impose their definition of the situation on others. The reverse also applies: those who cannot directly coerce others but still succeed in defining the situation (by rhetoric or whatever other means of persuasion) also to that extent dominate.

If everyone were cast in the same mold and had the same ideas, there could be no concept "truth." "Truth" requires "untruth,"

---

scribed as embarrassing. From this it can be deduced that he had never had occasion to speak the word until after he became so eminent that no one liked to correct him.

[2]"But it really does move!"

and because ideas are contested we need "objective truth," supposedly the product of dispassionate observation and reasoning. But political contests are anything but dispassionate and have little room for the kind of problem solving that lets us perform heart transplants or make computers or build better mousetraps; in those instances we know what we want, and the problem is to find the best means to achieve the end. But in political contests rationality is displaced because the contest is precisely about ends (values or interests) that are not agreed upon; as when it is argued that money spent on the armed services would have been better spent on schools and universities or medical research.

Yet even in politics we still search constantly for an objective reality, in the light of which to decide what should be done. Where could that reality be found?

Hard-Hat Truth

I will begin with a false start, because if I do not, someone will wonder how I came to overlook such an obvious solution. In fact, it is only half a false start (a mind-stopping confusion of metaphor that accords well with this topic).

> The process approach and action theory have tended toward an increasing emphasis on cognition, decision making and motivation. The materialist perspective has been left by the wayside. There are no end of analyses on how actors in political dramas manipulate symbols, rules, norms, or customs, but very little discussion is devoted to how they manipulate physical resources, or how they are affected by such resources. (Lewellen 1983:131)

In abandoning the "materialist perspective," which went well with my simple positivism, and putting "an increasing emphasis on cognition, decision making and motivation," I am probably alienating any reader who prefers, as I once did, to see politics as the study of ambitious men manipulating and at the same time being constrained by material resources. From that perspective material resources—such as the size of an army and its fire power and its air support, or such as money to buy time on television, or such as resources that come out of a pork barrel—are objective, real things in a real world, and open to accurate measurement without the risk of cultural distortion. They constitute laypeople's truth, the truth of experience, like Dr. Johnson proving the existence of matter by kicking a stone. Things are things, it is said, whatever the language or the culture. In this simple way relativism is banished and objective truth restored to its throne.

Of course material things are important, and political life is certainly more than political dramas and cultural performances. Words and symbols that stand for material things (words and symbols being the stuff of cognition and decisions and motivations) are not the same as the things themselves. To begin with, tokens are cheaply deployed (other things being equal), while material resources can be expensive. Military exercises conducted on a sand table (or nowadays by means of a computer) cost less in gasoline and ammunition and boot leather than the real thing. Second, as variables, material resources lend themselves more easily to factoring than do less tangible things such as decisions and motivations and morale. Numbers and quantities are tickets of admission to the real world; it is sometimes rashly said that numbers do not lie (just as guns do not kill people). Third—and here the argument begins to undermine itself—the real world is a *real* world and can turn out to be different from the *symbolic* world that is supposed to represent it. Predictions are confounded when God elects, as Voltaire suggested, *not* to be on the side of the big battalion.

At this stage, the pass has been partly sold. The hard, objective material environment is accessible to us as thinkers (or as ambitious people planning work on the world) only through symbols and schemas and representations. If the "real" world turns out through direct experience to be different from what we predicted, we still need symbols to make sense of the difference. Of course, there is a real world out there to be experienced, and in the last resort silk purses are not made out of sows' ears, and people get told to "put their money where their mouth is" and, if you believe Lincoln, that you cannot deceive all the people all the time. But perhaps the "last resort" is not unlike Keynes's "long run," when "we are all dead." Much that is important gets accomplished short of Judgment Day, through the skillful deployment of words and symbols.

Indeed, without such deployment nothing is likely to be done at all. Would-be leaders need to show some dexterity in handling symbols, rules, and norms before they can get their hands on material resources. Physical resources do not *alone* call the tune: what also matters is how people define the material environment, what possibilities they can see in it, what scruples they have about using it, and so on. More than that, even the manipulation of physical resources is often significant for the message it gives, as much as for its direct physical consequences. For that reason, Voltaire noted (referring to the unfortunate Admiral Byng, who was shot for failing to engage the French with sufficient zeal), the English think it "well from time to time to kill an admiral, to encourage the rest."

Thus the hard-hat version of truth, defined in simple terms as an underlying material reality, is partly unseated, because it is predictive only at the extremes (silk purses and sows' ears); a degree of relativism is restored.

I have several times suggested shelving the notion of *objective truth* and therefore *objective reality* (but still recognizing the rhetorical force of those phrases) and envisaging social interaction as a debate in which "truth" and "deceit" are adversaries. We already think of the tension between "truth" and "error" as the basis of scientific knowledge. Perhaps the tension between "truth" and "deceit" in a similar way is the basis of our political life (perhaps of all our social life), and life is itself a continuing contradiction between rival definitions of truth. The only world that then would be accessible to us would be a world conveyed in definitions and meanings; and "truth" would become "truths," referring to a plurality of contested coherence-truths. In other words, truth would be relative to particular systems and there would be no universal truth. Have we, then, solved the problem of objectivity by just walking round it?

Let us travel in that direction and see what happened to certain anthropologists (those of the hermeneutical or interpretive persuasion) who went down the same road, and let us ask what lessons we can derive from their experience to help us understand politics. What happened to those who reached the road's end is not wholly encouraging; the journey brings some benefits to the travelers (and to us), but also, in venturing close to the edge of absurdity, those who push on until they reach terminal postmodernism pay some far from trivial costs.

Relativism and Anthropology

Interpretive anthropologists, who have no fear of relativism, assert that it is a mistake to search in the sociocultural world for some kind of noncultural objectivity underlying or transcending different cultures; there are such things, but they have little relevance for the understanding of cultures. It follows from this that a correspondence theory of truth, which calls for an objective reality existing apart from and setting limits upon our cultural definitions of reality, should not be used to validate propositions about culture. Cultures are *sui generis* and are not a part of nature. Fire burns and water flows downhill and everywhere the human body deteriorates with age, but these and similar facts are merely the raw materials that each culture processes; other than in that way, they do not shape it.

In other words there is no point in searching, like a foolish positivist, for the *causes* of culture. The sociocultural world is sufficiently explained by the very act of analyzing it, in the same way that languages are explained by, among other procedures, syntactical analysis. We should look for *patterns*, not natural systems, Evans-Pritchard said, launching his parricidal assault on Radcliffe-Brown and on the "naive determinism" entailed in viewing societies as natural systems (1962). Natural laws and natural systems emerge from the kind of analysis done by scientists in the natural world, and such analysis is possible only because that world is not rendered unsystematic by a moral and symbolic dimension: planetary systems are not destabilized by the collective representations of the planets or by their scruples of conscience; nor, incidentally, do they tell lies.

So, if culture does not correspond with any natural world, how do you sort out the true descriptions from the false? How could one *pattern* be correct and another incorrect? The pattern that I see in the coals glowing in the fireplace is not the same as the one you see. Does it make sense to ask which one is valid? But perhaps the analogy is misleading. My description of a pattern in the fire may be deemed correct if the description accurately conveys what I see in the fire. That is where the correspondence is to be found. The correctness of a description depends upon a correspondence not with something that exists out in the natural world but with a mental representation, a pattern of thinking in someone's mind. In other words, it has "psychological reality." That, however, cannot be a final solution to the problem of separating cultural truth from cultural falsity. It is the difficulty with Bok's truth over again. We know what truth is ("everything that is the case"), but we still have to find a way to identify it. We know that the correct description is the one that has psychological reality, that accurately conveys what people think. But how to identify it?

The early Geertz (1966) introduced the idea that culture provides us with both "models of" and "models for" what goes on in the world. Therefore, in principle, since a "model for" is directive, its validity could be tested by seeing if it (a particular description of culture) correctly forecast (other things being equal) what people would do and say next. The description could be wrong; it could describe something that wasn't in people's minds at all. Eventually you would find this out, *if you decided to make the test*, in a standard empirical fashion, by making deductions and testing them against observed actions.

But later (1973:3–30), Geertz took a turn that subordinates the question of psychological reality. He suggested that the better cultural description is the one that is "thicker," which means the description that best conveys the rich complexity of meanings that actions or events imply for the actors—in other words, working out as fully as you can "what on earth must have been in their minds to make them behave that way."

But the problem of whether or not the thick description has psychological reality is still present. Thickness alone will not discriminate between what is an accurate description and what is not. Moreover, the thicker the description ethnographers provide, the less they seem to be concerned with testing for psychological reality. Energies seem to go more into thickening the description (uncovering its complex and, one hopes, elegant patterning) than into testing its accuracy by observing behavior. The risk then is that the writer is not uncovering the complexity at all but creating it, not interpreting but composing: "patterns of," perhaps (what the interpeter decides to see in the fire), but never "patterns for."

Thus, returning to the patterns in the fire, we have arrived at the terminus where postmodernist anthropology is located. Postmodernists do indeed insist that creative writing is exactly what anthropologists do and what they should do; and at that stage, of course, objectivity (truth by correspondence) has vanished.

How does one arrive in that strange land where ethnography, purportedly descriptive, has become a branch of fiction? Oddly enough, the trip starts with something that relativists, intent upon particular cultures, firmly deny: anthropology is a comparative discipline, seeking not only for what is different but also for what is shared between cultures. It is the study of *other* cultures, and therefore it is inevitably dominated by a strongly relativist tradition. But it is also directed toward the discovery of general patterns. This generality, which makes comparison possible, itself constitutes an underlying reality.

There are several candidates for the position of underlying reality: Marx's materialist base or a standard structure and capacities of the human mind or a standard psychophysiology that leads to standard psychological drives and sociological needs; *Culture* contrasted with cultures; and a variety of other postulated universals. The notion is not complicated. For example, given such needs as order, procreation, material necessities, and so forth, every culture must have some way of ministering to them. But different cultures create different kinds of institutions for these purposes: same problems, varying solutions.

The objection that interpretivists make to this search for generality is not that it is wrong but simply that it points in the wrong direction: away from what is "thick," from the rich complexity of particulars, and toward what is thin and simple and universal ("trivial" or "vacuous" are favored epithets; there is an obvious reason for avoiding "crass"). Truth, the interpretivists insist, is to be found by going in the other direction. The institutions—sets of beliefs and values and their corresponding customs—constitute, when put together, a richly interconnected pattern, in which any one institution acquires its meaning only when set in the context of the others. In that sense cultural anthropology has to be relativist: each culture is distinct and is comprehended as a whole. The truth of one culture is not the truth of another culture, and other cultures, so far as we are concerned, are *other* cultures.

So far so good. But what has happened to the venture into comparison? Things that have nothing in common cannot be compared. But do different cultures really have nothing in common? To argue that calls for some quick sophistry: *petitio principii*. First, one assumes that human conduct and its associated values and beliefs are exclusively the product of cultures (*not* of a pan-human Culture). That we all share the need to eat and sleep and have sex and enjoy companionship is not denied; it is merely dismissed as being irrelevant to the understanding of particular cultures. This is to beg the question at the outset, but let it pass: questions always get begged at the outset. (Openly begged, the answer is presented as self-evident, an "axiom.")

Second, the reasoning continues, cultures are different from one another and are mutually incomprehensible in the same sense that languages (language, obviously, is a cultural manifestation) are different and mutually incomprehensible.[3] It then follows that the act of translation from one culture to another is not merely difficult—every anthropologist knows that—but inherently impossible. Each language is a part of that unique and intrinsic whole that constitutes a culture, and to describe one culture in the language of another culture is to do it violence. Therefore the enterprise of anthropology—to describe and understand other cultures—is essentially a fraud. One can describe one's own encounter with another culture, but what is then being described is, at best, the encounter, more often not even the encounter but rather one or another aspect of the writer's own self, certainly never the "other" culture.

The argument is then reinforced *ad hominem* by accusing those who deny it of moral inadequacy. Ironically the case rests upon an implicit appeal to an ethical principle, presumed to be universal but in fact rather specific to our culture and its congeners, and even there not always practiced: it is a sin to treat others as instruments. The case is made like this. In a relativist world each culture is self-contained and unique. Comparison is impossible because there is no common basis on which to make the comparison. To insist that there is a basis of commonness is to

---

[3]Methodological folklore for anthropology graduate students in postwar Oxford recognized the cultural embeddedness of language by insisting that it was wiser *not* to learn the native language before going to the field. Dictionaries and grammars, compiled by missionaries and administrators, would be culturally biased. This arrogant advice was often virtue cut from the cloth of necessity, because there were no grammars, no dictionaries, and no teachers. When there were teachers, moreover, they were usually to be found not in Oxford but, *in partibus infidelium*, in that land of the heathens the University of London.

be an intellectual imperialist, attributing to others—and therefore imposing on them—the values and beliefs of our own culture. Therefore not only is translation impossible, but attempts at translation are immoral, inasmuch as they violate "native life." Consider the following from a leading writer in the postmodern persuasion in anthropology:

> [The metaphor of translation] begs the question of the source of the authority that enables the ethnographer to speak for the native, no matter how it is done. Moreover, it makes explicit the motivation of ethnography, which, like the metaphor of translation itself, seeks to dominate difference by means of identities or equivalences which make native life fit the civilized contours of our own discourse, make it palatable to our sapience, and amenable to our interests. (Tyler 1987:96)

It follows that if one wanted a "true" ethnography of—let us say—the Todas who live in the Nilgiri Hills in India, it would have to be written in the Toda language.[4]

There is in this, as in other postmodernist writing, a romanticism that sees evil in uniformity, in regularity, in order itself. The metaphor in the phrase "dominate difference by means of identities or equivalences" discloses the writer's agenda in that very word "dominate." He might have said "seeks to find similarity in difference," but he chose not to, so that his firm stand against totalitarianism, in whatever form, should be properly advertised. I, too, as by now the reader of this essay must perceive, have most sympathy with those who distrust authority, but not when they so blatantly confuse the issue and not when they inadvertently disembowel themselves with their own rhetoric.

Yes, translation "dominates." In other words the idioms and values of the receiving language must not merely be taken into account but must also be allowed to set the style. Not to do so is

---

[4]Tyler may have a point. There are paragraphs in Rivers's famous monograph on the Todas where this does indeed appear to be the case, virtually all the nouns being in the Toda language.

violate one's audience, to fail to reach them, to behave in a way that is not "palatable to [their] sapience, and amenable to [their] interests"—in other words, to offend ("palatable") and to injure ("interests") the reader. It is no less wrong to make instruments of sapient readers than of "natives" (whose "sapience," if they have any, the postmodernists assume we would find unsavory). Notice, second, that the issue is not raised over translations from French to Chinese or Japanese to German; only from "native life" into a metropolitan language such as English. Translation, which the politically innocent may have thought no more than a search for the best equivalents, the product of careful and reasoned compromise, becomes the imposition of uniformities, the cultural domination of one language by another, a simple transformation of the colonial situation, offered not as a metaphor but as an instance of totalitarianism.[5]

Mostly this seems to me self-indulgent moralizing. It is the kind of conscience that makes speaking-socialists out of rich men's sons, venting oedipal anger into the public domain, beating one's breast for sins committed by the fathers, confessing without making restitution, foregrounding the "I" and making the "Other" nothing more than an instrument for catharsis. So easily the writing descends into poetic nonsense, if not humbug; a concentration on trivia; indignation run riot in an ivory tower. Of course native cultures have been misrepresented, even travestied. But colonists and colonial powers—totalitarian governments everywhere—have provided many less trivial reasons for righteous anger than cultural misrepresentation. Of course cultural misrepresentation is wrong, but . . . Tell it to the Tasmanians![6]

The postmodernists also spike themselves with their own rhetoric. The same verdict that they pass on anthropologists who

[5]One wonders what totalitarian violence was done to English when missionaries translated the King James version into Kui, the language of the Konds.
[6]The aboriginal inhabitants of Tasmania are but one of many populations wiped out by colonists.

lack the "authority" (and the ability) to speak for the Other, can be entered on the relativist writers' own accounts of their encounters with other cultures. More than that, the argument will also apply to communication between subdisciplinary cultures within anthropology, and if we all carry, existentialist fashion, our own idioverses[7] (our personal way of looking at the world), it would follow that each postmodernist (being at the extreme and therefore ultimately solipsist wing of relativism) must constitute a culture on his or her own, and therefore does not have much capacity to understand or interpret even the writings of other postmodernists, let alone what is written by anthropologists of other persuasions. A cheap shot, perhaps, but on target, for one can further deduce not only that postmodernists will misunderstand and misrepresent the anthropological enterprise as others practice it but also that their own writings will often be somewhat incomprehensible to others, certainly outside and even inside postmodernism. This is indeed sometimes the case. A modest footnote at the end of an article by Fischer (1986:233) indicates that his colleagues, presumably sympathetic, did not understand his first draft and that he had therefore "reverted to a more traditional authorial guiding voice."[8] The situation is aptly conveyed in the following quotation:

> Ethnography is the endorphin of culture, an intertextual practice which, by means of an allegorizing identity, anesthetizes us to the other's difference. Its other is a same, made so by a process of double occultation, for the ethnographic text can represent the other as difference only inasmuch as it makes itself occult, and can only reveal itself inasmuch as it makes the other occult, which is the condition of modernism. Postmodern ethnography must be another kind of intertextuality whose project is not to reveal the other in univocal descriptions which allegorically identify the other's difference as our interest. It must be instead, a fantasy of identities, a plurivocal evocation of difference making a unity in

[7]Schwartz 1978.
[8]An essay by Kevin Birth brought this to my attention.

fantasy that mimics on every page the rationalism that seems to inform it, and reveals between every line the difference it conceals in every word, that it might speak not for the other "for us," but let the other's voice be heard, too, and not just "for us," but "for us both." (Tyler 1987:102)

True, indeed; and out goes plain description with the rest of the ethnograhic trash! Instead we write fiction; we are free to create, to mimic, to play games, to be "ludic," and if in the course of the creative performance we happen also to be ludicrously inaccurate, that is of no account. All that can fault such writing is an aesthetic lapse, a failure of taste. The reader, since this is fantasy and not description, not interpretation but composition, has already agreed to suspend disbelief and to forget reality testing. She has not come to learn, only to be entertained.

Tyler's book is called *The Unspeakable*, but it is in fact eminently speakable, some of it being written (but not typeset) in blank verse. When read aloud (try the "endorphin" quotation), it reveals many pleasing sermonlike cadences, Ciceronian, grandiloquent. It is, however, unlike most of Cicero, difficult to follow, at least if one looks for a reasoned argument rather than rhetoric. It is a sectarian book, a scripture that insists on (but does not much argue for) its own version of *the* truth, and presumably "everyone that is of the truth heareth [Tyler's] voice." It is a political discourse, an extended tract written to convert the disciplinary heathens (or at least to annoy them) and to encourage true-believers.[9]

But perhaps I should not throw that particular stone, demanding systematic argument in place of persuasion, asking for clarity. Insisting on clarity may, after all, be just a rhetorical trick to make other people translate their ideas into your language, where

[9]It is possible, of course, that Tyler's book is ironic, a joke, a deliberate but veiled "disoccultation," a covert deconstruction and therefore destruction of the genre, a warning to us all of what awaits if, risking *lues postmoderna*, we frequent their ill-famed houses, losing our academic virtue and soiling the purity of our science.

they cannot be expressed without serious distortion. I suppose, in any case, Tyler could reasonably say that to ask for that kind of univocality is precisely to beg the question; there are no reasoned arguments, only rhetoric, and the very phrase "reasoned argument" is itself a piece of rhetoric. The theory, it seems, is as insulated, impenetrable, and self-sealing as the cultures it hypothesizes.

All this is somewhat bizarre and, to my mind, self-contradictory insofar as the logical outcome of extreme relativism (a silent conversation with oneself) is a course of action which relativists themselves do not and could not follow. When they are not sermonizing, they too write books about other cultures, and these books are not cut whole-cloth out of their own selves. Once down from the pulpit, they too have to settle (as every sensible person always has done) for less-than-accurate ethnographies because any account of another culture is filtered through the assumptions and prejudices of the anthropologist's own culture (and of his own psyche, I might add, suggesting that culture is not the only determinant of behavior). It is also filtered through whatever syntactical framework, whatever paradigms, the writer uses. Who would deny that? The only wisdom is to follow Adlai Stevenson (if this is what he meant) and strive constantly to be aware of one's biases and to be open about them.

Of course ethnographies are flawed and contain mistakes and misrepresentations, innocent or otherwise. Certainly the picture that comes over to the reader is shaped—and inevitably so—by whatever is the writer's guiding rhetoric and guiding ideology, and those who follow other ideologies and other rhetorics will call it distortion. The natives, Renato Rosaldo tells us (1987), either cannot recognize themselves in ethnographic writing or see themselves caricatured. Old anthropology, structural-functional anthropology, positive anthropology, Radcliffe-Brown and all those other not-thick ethnographers, he says, abstract away the rich complexity of native life. Of course they do. How else is anything known or written except by abstraction? Even the thickest description must be an abstraction. In the end Rosaldo's objection can be no more than a statement of his preference and of what, in a particular case, he claims to be the native preference. To tell it all is, in a quite literal way, unthinkable. Partiality (in either sense) is inevitable; it surely does not render the entire enterprise a fraud. If the beef is sometimes overdone, will you become a vegetarian? If the chef regularly fails to produce perfection, are you ready to starve?

If we draw back from the extremes of postmodernism and contemplate instead "ordinary" relativism—the notion that our job is to find Evans-Pritchard's "patterns" and describe them as thickly as we can—what is to be said? First, there could be no anthropology of any kind without such descriptive analysis; obviously one cannot compare cultures without first describing them. Second, the relativist or pluralist creed constitutes an always needed reminder that it is foolish to think that others must see themselves as we see them and it is *very* foolish to conclude, when we find that they construe the world differently, that they are stupid or wicked. Anthropologists seldom fall into that last error, except when they are talking about each other. But the former error, inadvertent projection of one's own culture, is a constant occupational hazard. Third—and this is a small pat on the back for postmodernists—their deconstructive habit of scrutinizing other peoples' ethnographies for evidence of bias, intellectual or otherwise, reinforces an entirely warranted demand for reflexivity, self-examination, self-criticism, and by implication, the production of something better.[10] The irony of the matter is that critical scrutiny and improved understanding even of texts (let alone of social life as it is directly experienced) is severely inhibited by relativist assumptions that make it hard to separate the better from the worse. Without doing that, how is one to know what is an improvement? I will come to that in a moment.

"Relativism" and "antirelativism" (the ante has been upped by

[10]They seem less than gratified when their own writings are given similar treatment. See the pained replies to Sangren 1988.

Geertz, who coined "anti-anti-relativism") present themselves as another of those dichotomous extremes (like "truth" and "deceit"), and if I am to be true to my own philosophy, neither of them could alone represent the anthropological experience. My truth (my syntactical system) lies between them (as, I believe, all but the craziest contestants[11] would admit once outside the debating chamber). In other words, most people operate with a conceptual framework that is a compromise between the two extremes, thus transforming them from contradictories to complementaries. There is no other *practical* way to proceed; once one gets down from the pulpit, the need for action (in this case the need to communicate across cultures) shatters rigid ideologies (in this case the dogma that each culture is one of a kind).

The issue, of course, is not decided once and for all by that piece of pragmatism. My problem is to understand what "truth" and "untruth" have to do with the distribution of power, and to explain why we cling so resolutely to the notion of absolute truth, refusing to contemplate its illusory nature. It is still possible that one of the truth frameworks (relativism or antirelativism; truth-by-coherence or truth-by-correspondence) may be more effective than the other in understanding the use in politics of "truth" and "untruth" and of their many substitutes.

Ethics and Epistemology

There is, as I have just said, a difficulty with relativism in the social sciences (or with hermeneutic or interpretive anthropology): its practitioners seem to have no clear way to decide

[11]Quick access to each opposing position is to be found in Geertz 1984 and Spiro 1986. Tempered statements appear in Keesing 1987 and Strathern 1987. See their references, and especially the commentaries following the latter two essays, to find some of the less-tempered arguments. The debate in anthropology represents a tiny corner of a vast arena in literature and in the philosophy of the social sciences.

between alternatives, because they do not see any need to do so. When there are different and incompatible versions, either of the way the world is or of the way the world should be, the question of deciding between them, of ranking them as true or false, right or wrong, is not relevant, because for a relativist cultures are made up of meanings, which are not constrained by an objective reality, and of moral judgments, which are not absolute.

In the case of meanings, for example, does anything in the world of nature anchor the meaning of the plus sign to the operations it signifies? Of course not; the link is one of convention. Meanings, under those conditions, cannot be objectively correct or incorrect, any more than nonpropositional things, like a wish or a feeling, could be correct or incorrect: they just *are*. White is the color of mourning in Hindu India: black in most of the Western world. These conventions are like words and phrases in languages, which are self-contained systems of meaning. One can, of course, verify in a perfectly "objective" fashion that for all qualified speakers of Italian *gatto* means *cat*: intersubjectivity is obectivity. But it would make no sense to ask if the Italian language is objectively correct when it uses the word *gatto* to refer to a cat. These are Cherry's syntactical systems: truth is not an absolute but is relative to the system.

Then, the prophet of disaster says (stepping swiftly out of epistemology into ethics and talking not about the way the world is but about the way it should be), if everything is relative, we will not know right from wrong. Morality has then become a mere convention, not an absolute. No one wants to believe the dismal prophet until word gets out that Paul de Man, a trendsetter in literary deconstructionism (a movement from which the anthropological postmodernists get much of their inspiration), was a wartime Nazi collaborator, writing anti-Semitic essays in a Belgian newspaper. Therefore, one may rashly conclude, since deconstructionism goes with anti-Semitism, relativism destroys morality.

The argument has considerable rhetorical force in most circles at the present day, but logically it fails. First, it begs the question of anti-Semitism's status as a (negative) moral absolute. Evidently it was not such an absolute for Paul de Man. Second, granting that anti-Semitism is abhorrent, the argument is weak because it assumes that the gun (relativism) is to blame, and not the person. Of course, it may well be that relativism, like a gun, makes it easier to do bad things. But moral judgments apply only to intentional actions, and instruments are neutral; fire is harmful or helpful, depending on how it is used. Third, even if it could be shown that relativism was ethically disastrous, not much could be done about it, since, unlike guns, value differences are a part of the human condition, and despite the efforts of politicians and other true-believers, value differences (unlike guns) cannot be legislated out of circulation.

But is there really such an ethical problem? Logically there are no good grounds for allowing Dismal Jimmy to jump from epistemology to morality. There is, of course, a connection between *ought* and *is*, because it is illogical to enjoin conduct that cannot be performed. But that apart, the way things are cannot *directly* condition the way things should be. What is desired is not necessarily a guide to what is desirable, as every undergraduate who has written an essay on John Stuart Mill well knows. Probably every culture that ever was has its quota of bigotry, but bigotry is still wrong. Moral judgments are our *judgments*, not facts of nature; they are matters of opinion. We can prove that most Americans believe that eating people is wrong, but we cannot prove that eating people *is* wrong: we can only assert it or take it on faith. The "ought" cannot be derived from the "is" (Hume 1940:3.165–78).

Moral principles, in other words, can only be secured in their own right, and the test of correspondence with an objective reality cannot apply. If you must anchor your moral principles and make them absolutes, you can say they are innate (or, to put it another way, divinely ordained) and then face the problem of explaining why some people seem not to share those principles. (A common solution is to say that people like that are not really people; they are subhuman.) Alternatively, you can leave the principles relatively unanchored and, in a kind of moral version of coherence-truth, agree that moral is no more than what the consensus in any particular society says is moral—a position that is, to say the least, uncomfortable, given our psychological need for certainty (not to speak of the bizarre conduct that certain Others reckon to be morally acceptable).

Deconstructionism does only half the job (and, in any case, is concerned more with ethics than with epistemology); it tells others what they must not believe but not what they should believe. That style is mostly in the demolition business, destroying ideologies by revealing their hidden agendas. For sure its proponents claim a commendable antipathy toward authoritarianism, but clearing the ground is only the first part of what has to be done. Where is the construction? "Versions of the truth" in politics are designs for taking action. Destroy all designs for action and there will be no action: in other words, nihilism. The solution, obviously, is not total demolition but constructive criticism: eliminate the bad and preserve the good. But you still need some way of telling good and bad apart.

All that still leaves hanging the epistemological question "How does one select between incompatible versions of the truth, of the way the world is?" In principle one way to test a version of sociocultural truth (asking whether it is *correct*, not whether it is morally acceptable) is, as I said earlier, to measure its capacity to forecast conduct (that is, not all behavior but culturally conditioned behavior). That procedure does not solve the problem of moral relativism, but it does provide a criterion by which to distinguish between accurate and inaccurate descriptions of values and beliefs. But as I said earlier, the anti-antirelativists walk away from that solution. Perhaps it is too obvious, or tainted with positivism. Perhaps it is the case that the thicker the descriptive analysis, the more complexity it folds into itself, and the harder it then becomes to devise any test that would link it to conduct. The process starts with what people do and say, but then, as the perceptions get richer and denser and more convoluted, more satisfactorily "thick" (maybe also more imaginative and more creative), the ethnography has "lift-off" and is not designed for reentry into a real world. At that point the question "Is that what they really think?" would surely be considered crass.

Geertz (1984) finds other ways of answering. Tilting vigorously at the windmills of antirelativism, he displays a talent, rarely found among anthropologists and not at all in his opponents, for sustained derision ("Dracula" and the like)—a rhetoric surely made easier by doom-struck antirelativist hyperbole. Then, when the time comes to drop the ridicule and produce his "truth," he shifts into ethics and the reader gets no more than an elaborate apodictic assertion that relativism has not stopped people ("and indeed I myself") from commitment; evidently he knows right from wrong and, it seems to be implied, truth from error. Perhaps he has access to a kind of poetic truth, which is its own guarantor. But this is like Bok's version of a clear-cut lie: you will know one when you meet one. *How* you will know it, Geertz does not explain. But neither does anyone else, presumably because ethical conviction cannot rest on an epistemological base and because, in this particular matter, the epistemological foundations for truth seem anything but secure.

No more need be said here on the question of ethical commitment. But the epistemological problem remains unsolved and we have not found a way to bring hermeneutical ethnography (and our own inquiry into power and deceit) out of orbit. So let us look for reentry, a way of getting safely back to the ground. (Of course, in politics it may be that once in orbit means always in orbit or burnup on reentering the real world. At least there is that tendency: think of Hitler or of such would-be charismatic leaders in Africa as Nkrumah.)[12]

[12]Both these men seem to have been deranged by their own charisma. Fest (1975) provides a readable and authoritative account of Hitler. Lacouture (1970) has a chapter on Nkrumah (Ghana's first head of state).

Where Are the Brakes?

For sure, the world of politics makes no sense at all without the notion of relativism. It is a world of plural understandings and plural moralities and a marked scarcity of absolutes, rich in *asserted* absolutes but poor in *agreed* absolutes. At first sight, politicians operate in an arena of independent and uncommunicable ideologies, of syntactical systems, each with its own truths, not unlike cultures as the relativists see cultures. So let us begin by asking what can be learned by making that comparison.

The benign commonsensical interpretivist anthropology, where Geertz cultivates his garden, immediately suggests one striking difference. Political ideologies are anything but thick descriptive analyses. They abhor complexity, resist qualification, refuse exceptions, and reject contradiction. They have a penchant for the elementary, whether forms or structures or systems. That they do is not surprising: politics look to persuasion, and the quality of simplicity is exactly what is required to move people into action.

So much for Geertz. But what of the harsher domains of postmodernism, where solipsism rules and cultures talk only to themselves? What does that image suggest about political ideologies? Are communism and free-market capitalism self-insulating? Are Marx and Milton Friedmann monolingual, using mutually incomprehensible languages, unable to communicate, there being no common premises from which to reason dialectically?

Sometimes it looks that way. Often political discourse is a matter of ideologues talking less *to* each other than *at* each other. True-believers in one ideology have trouble communicating with those of a different persuasion and often seem not to be trying to understand any position other than their own: at the level of debate they end up, whatever the facade of reason, essentially shouting slogans and abuse. This happens because political ide-

119

ologies, like other dogmas, claim to have an exclusive handle on *the* truth, and therefore to be unique. If they are unique, they must by definition be incomparable. But that is sophistry. The uniqueness is no more than a politician's claim: it belongs in the domain of rhetoric, a matter not of plain description but of persuasion. It is not the case that political ideologies are unique, only that their upholders say they are, because "unique" suggests "having no equal" and therefore "superior."

Ideologies can be presented as unique only *at the level of ideological statement*, abstracted from and protected from the erosions that practice inflicts on the smooth surface of theory. Left as forms, they can claim to be immaculate; turned into levers—instruments for acting on the world—they are inevitably compromised.[13] Place them in the world where decisions have to be made and implemented—that is, make them *practical* ideologies—and not one of them can operate without diluting its purity. (In those conditions they do have a tendency to become "thick" by taking into account more and more variables). In other words, purportedly unique political ideologies must have some features in common precisely because they are practical, intended to guide action in a world of problems, the similarity of which puts similar constraints upon all of them. Then the ideologies are comparable, at the very least with respect to the success they have in dealing with practical problems. Reentry, in short, is a periodic requirement. To stay in orbit all the time is to become "just talk."

To that extent ideologies, when they are transformed into programs or even policies, are somewhat constrained by a real world. More than that, ideologies are in competition and therefore are constrained by the debate that they have with one another. Communist ideology exists in contradiction to capitalist ideology, each addressing the other's inadequacies while tailoring its own perfection. Beyond the ideologies are the people. Communists interact with, come into conflict with, and sometimes

---

[13]"Form" and "lever" are taken from the felicitous Geertz 1988:125.

come to terms with capitalists, and vice versa. In short, the very coexistence of rival ideologies, together with the purported guidance they offer in dealing with the real world, ensures that they cannot be self-contained and unique: they must not only be aware of each others' values (if only to combat them better) but also make compromises. Opposing political ideologies are not like hypothetically unique cultures, first, because they are *practical* ideologies and, second, because they are *opposing*, not merely intellectually incompatible.

The same is not true of hermeneutical interpretations. The relativists in anthropology, I have said, do not put their descriptions to any rigorous test of praxis. If their interpretations are wildly out of line, then (being merely scholars) they still do not have a problem; their statements are not guides for action in the world. At most they are like realistic novels, retrospectively validated by the reader's contemplative sense of "that's the way it probably is." Alternatively, they have no content that could be "validated" and are compositions to be appreciated, like a poem or a piece of music, for their form alone. Could that also be true of political statements that are designed to direct policy? It could not be: politicians and their arguments are in the real world of substance and consequence, not form alone. Social and political life is a contest between adversaries whose aim is to exert leverage on the world by making their own goals, plans, and policies prevail as "truth", while those of their opponents are dismissed as "error" or, when the chance offers, "deceit."

Such contests go on and never come to an end, because when one battle is ended another begins, and the arena is never emptied of contenders. But the process is not uninterrupted; it is punctuated by decisions. Sometimes there is a compromise. At other times one "truth" defeats another "truth," and a choice is in fact made between different versions of the truth. Then should the winning version be called "objective" or "real" truth? If so, right is might. The winner is ipso facto (which comes near to saying "objectively") the better version. The best truth, like the best man, has won, and truth is then the plaything of power.

121

As an explanation of why one "truth" prevails, this one is often undeniable; remember Galileo. But remembering Galileo and his incautious (if apocryphal) obstinacy, I am uncomfortable with the argument because what in Galileo's case was politically "true" was also objectively false; the earth does go round the sun. To insist *in an unqualified way* that truth is always what prevails politically would put us in the stocks with the man who said "Fifty million Frenchmen can't be wrong."

Then how should it be qualified? Consider first a more detailed version of how one "truth" defeated the others. It did so because it had superior techniques. The winning side had the edge, perhaps rhetorically (better public relations, better audience research, better speakers, more time on television) and materially (more money to bribe voters, more thugs to intimidate the opposition, and so forth). But why did *those* techniques prevail? The answer to that question must invoke an objective world, the existence of which causes one solution to be more effective than another. Certain truths—perhaps in politics all truths—are instructions on how to get things done. They are designs for manipulating people and resources in contexts that are to some degree beyond control, and to which the designs must be adapted. These contexts include, of course, beliefs and values—"what is really in their minds to make them behave that way." If the designs are not adapted to the contexts, they fail: they are proved to be "untrue." We are like sailing ships, and the designs are charts that enable us (within limits) to steer a course, but only if we take account of objective constraints such as the wind and the currents. Action and the experience it brings determine the fate of ideas.

This argument suggests a plausible (but regrettably unsound) conclusion: grand designs like capitalism or communism or Islam or Christianity, or lesser designs like functionalism or structuralism or postmodernism, and other such basic lies, might all in the end be subject to the same kind of empirical test as is the plan to warm your hands by putting them into the fire. The ultimate control on a design (that is, a purported truth) is whether or not it copes with a real world of fundamental problems: food, shelter, sex and reproduction, the universality of death and suffering, companionship, order, creativity, and whatever else it is that marks the human condition. Truth, perhaps, is what works. Saying that, I feel instant discomfort, but not because the statement is false. We do have such needs. Nor is it vacuous: human needs can be specified in formidable detail whether in scientific research or in that recent cornucopia of books on what to eat, how to enjoy sex, and how to "relate" to other people or how to do them down. The misgivings arise because people do not think in that way about the constraints of an objective reality. Remember we are seeking an epistemological foundation for basic lies: how they do, or do not, get tested; whether those that prevail do so because they are anchored in reality or for some other reason that is unconnected with reality. Cherry's layman, if asked why one design for living (one syntactical system) is better than another, would need considerable Socratic coaching before he came up with—and accepted—such yardsticks as shelter, sex, or sociality. In other words, the *everyday* empiricism and the notion of an objective universal truth cannot originate from a contemplation of physical, neuropsychological, or sociological needs. So how does one account for that straightforward "hard-hat" conviction in everyday life that facts are facts and sooner or later everyone comes up against reality?

Empirical knowledge of that reality is part of everyone's experience, although not necessarily an everyday experience. We live and learn partly by trial and error, on the job. This is not the world of science, which thinks far ahead of action and is continually asking questions and doubting. Rather it is the world of the artisan or craftsman who works with something quite close to *habitus*—that is, he does not need to think much about what to do[14]—until something goes wrong; only then does he work

---

[14]There are still good cooks who have not learned from a recipe book. Question: "How long do you cook it?" Answer: "Until it's done, of course!" A similar reliance on *habitus* appears in the horror a committee displays when someone suggests abandoning a basic formula for distributing scarce goods. Sensible committees countenance only incremental change.

out how it could be differently and better done.[15] Of course, experimental tendencies vary from one person to another, from one age to another, and from one culture to another. Experience stands ready to teach everywhere, but all pupils are not equally receptive. But there can be no pupils anywhere outside the madhouse who are entirely unfamiliar with trial-and-error procedures and their entailed notion of a recalcitrant physical reality.

The everyday notion of an objective and universal truth, however, also has another and very different origin: a universal psychological need to be sure of something, to put an end to the questioning, to know where one stands. This need is manifested by the unquestioned dogma, the scripture, the eternal verity, God's truth, in fact any belief that is maintained in defiance of experience and is protected from the test of trial and error. Included in that list is the basic lie. A basic lie, remember, is not publicly presented as a *lie*, as a pretense or a convention, but rather as reality: not someone's idea of the way the world is, but the way the world in fact is. Remember the craftsman who does not question his techniques until something goes wrong. Basic lies are doubly strengthened by building in a pretense that they cannot go wrong, together with rules for misreading the evidence when they do go wrong, what Evans-Pritchard (1937:348) called a "secondary elaboration of belief." They may also be protected by powerful people, whose privileges the lies support.

From those two mutually contradictory sources "layman's truth" emerges: hard experience, on the one hand, and, on the other, dogma, scripture, the held-on-faith, socially fortified "truth." The latter brings me to the second reason for doubting that political and other ideologies can be tested by hand-in-the-fire procedures. The notion seriously misrepresents the testing process in all cases of political deception, but especially basic lies. There is no simple and more or less immediately conclusive experiment like hands-in-the-fire or eating poisonous mushrooms.[16] The test of a basic lie is rarely immediate; often it is over

[15]These ideas come from Gellner 1985:101–27.
[16]As I write Eastern Europe and the Soviet Union have been two months in

124

the long haul, and the results may be visible only in the hindsight of history. The objective conditions that caused Germany to lose two wars or Athens first to create and then to destroy an empire are clearer now than at the time, and also are clearer to those whose interests are not committed to the struggle or who are not being intimidated by beneficiaries of the basic lie.

In short, when basic lies (which, as I said, masquerade as basic truths) are questioned, they are not so much tested as *contested*. Hand-in-the-fire is a simple test. The fire has nothing to gain or lose, does not know the difference between warmth and third-degree burns, and does not devise plans to fudge the result. Now think about the Orissa coalition; there was no simple unequivocal experiment available to decide whether the coalition would be good or bad for the state and its people, and even if there had been, the side that stood to lose by the test would surely have found a way to declare it invalid. Plainly we are back in a subjective world of opinions, claims, and of course power.

The conclusion seems inevitable. Objective conditions may indeed set limits to the use of untruths (ordinary lies or basic lies) but the limits are so very wide that they are usually predictors only "in the long run." Furthermore, objective truth is rarely a primary concern for politicians. When politicians assert that something is true, or even when they asks themselves whether or not it is true, they mostly have an eye not on anything in the objective world but more on rhetoric and persuasion. "Will it fly?" takes precedence over "Is it true?" In any case, even if politicians sincerely believe what they say (like Adlai Stevenson, one hopes, insisting that truth must prevail over false ideologies), both the consequences of the claim and the intentions of the speakers are mostly in the domain of rhetoric. The words do not primarily convey a truth (or a falsehood) about an objective world; instead they serve to persuade people toward actions and

---

turmoil. I cannot, unlike most commentators, see these events as a conclusive hand-in-the-fire test, which communism failed; in a short time all may look different. If it is a conclusive test, then it is a slow one. Those people have had their hands in the fire for more than forty years.

attitudes. The empirical test that politicians would think relevant concerns the capacity of propositions to persuade, not their correspondence with some objective reality. Hitler, for example, surely an expert in the field, concluded that big, bold, spectacular lies were more effective than small, cautious lies.

The entire ethos of politics, the characteristic spirit of those struggling for power, pushes people away from rationality, from matching means to ends, from reality testing. I do not mean that there are no calculating politicians, estimating relative resources, biding their time, planning their strategies, and so forth; of course there are. But I do mean that, exactly because politics constitute a contest, there is a continuous incentive to reach beyond culturally constituted rationality, to do the unexpected, to innovate, to be audacious, and, above all, to be deceitful. That is the way to throw an opponent off balance without having to use force.

Untruth—the whole range from outright lies to fantasy—is the mover. Untruth, in the form of a basic lie, is also the best we can do in politics to find a place to stand. But when we want to move the world (that is, to destabilize some basic lie), we need deceit and fictions. To say it again, deceit and fictions are Max Weber's magic—creativity, imagination, fantasy, ingenuity, charisma—all those denials of the iron cage which he saw in rational bureaucracy and which are constitutive of any basic lie. Francis Bacon saw some of this when he wrote that "truth is a naked and open day-light, that doth not show the masks and mummeries and triumphs of the world, half so stately and daintily as candlelights." Or this: "A mixture of a lie doth ever add pleasure." Then, landing exactly on target, he asks if all untruth were removed, would it not "leave the minds of a number of men poor shrunken things, full of melancholy and indisposition, and unpleasing to themselves?" (1909:7–8). Is that not a good description of the wholly regulated citizen, the civic automaton who does not know the pleasure of fantasy and deceit?

Does it also follow that the politician who "clings everlastingly to the truth" (1) is doing nothing of the sort because he is in fact clinging to a basic lie and (2) is headed for disaster because sooner or later the world will change and make that basic lie a formula for self-extinction? I think it does, if "truth" is indeed illusory and nothing but a basic lie. But is that pessimistic message all that emerges from this book? I hope not.

Let us go over the argument again. On the one side is truth; on the other side is untruth. Untruth has three main forms: deceit, error, and fiction. We have no difficulty in saying what each of these four things are. Truth is the statement of anything that is the case. Deceit is the deliberate statement of what is known not to be the case; and so is fiction. They differ because deceit is directed toward controlling or manipulating the other person, whereas fiction is for entertainment, delectation, and perhaps, in a sense, for education—broadening the mind. Error is the unwitting assertion of what is not the case.

Notice that all four words presuppose a communication or interaction. All my arguments are addressed to that interaction. My concern is not *directly* with a relationship between a proposition and an objective world to which the proposition refers or between a proposition and the degree of consensus it commands in a particular group. I am interested in understanding how each of these notions of "truth" and their entailed "untruths" influence communication between persons. In other words, we are not directly answering Pilate's question "What is Truth?" Rather, we are asking how the concept "truth" and its opposite "untruth" (in its several forms) are used to manipulate an interaction and define a situation. There is, of course, implied in this procedure, an answer to Pilate: "Truth is an illusion."

The manipulation of social interaction would not be the artful thing it is, if truth were not an illusion and if we had a practical and objective way to resolve the epistemological problem, a litmus test that would tell us with absolute certainty into which of the four categories any particular statement fell. We do not have such a test; we do not even have a way of deciding which (if either) of the two kinds of test for truth—truth by correspondence or truth by coherence, objective truth set against "intersubjectivity is objectivity"—is preferable. In practice we compromise between foundationalism (God's objective truth) and relativism (the fifty million Frenchmen who can't be wrong). But neither of those positions is philosophically comfortable, and both emerge as ideologies to be asserted or defended rather than as demonstrated truths.

In other words, the only way in which we can understand "truth" and "untruth" is to see them as rhetoric, as concepts used primarily for persuasion. They are political words, weapons for use in competition for power. In that context "truth" and "untruth" represent a tension, a tug of war, a dialogue between adversaries, who use these words in the contest, each striving to make their own ideas and values prevail.

Contest is the central feature of politics, but there would not be such a contest if we did not have so strong a need to wrap ourselves around with a *habitus*, to find "the truth," to find a place on which to stand, to settle comfortably with one answer and relieve ourselves of the anxiety aroused by questioning, doubt, and uncertainty. We are, so to speak, sitting ducks for political rhetoric. We resent the notion that the politicians' "truth" is illusory, that it is a "basic lie." Like the craftsman, well versed in his habitual techniques, we are reluctant to abandon them, even when we know that things are not going well.

The very nature of political interaction pushes us back from any serious and sustained effort to ask questions and so find the kind of scientific truth that goes into building bridges, controlling erosion, or even growing tomatoes. In that respect politics brings about *dis*education, discouraging thought and providing authorized, preprocessed answers. The scientific kind of inquiry—how means and ends relate to each other—is inappropriate exactly because politics concern contested values, not the means to attaining some accepted value. Politics, in other words, can never be like a natural science. Politicians, who are by definition contestants to make one or another value prevail, cannot avoid moral questions. Even when they take trouble to find the "facts," it is only so that they can better impose their own definitions of the right and the good. (In that respect, to the extent that politicians provoke debate about values, they are educators.)

This book also is a political act. Certainly I have been at pains to describe how I think the political and social world works and to provide supporting evidence. But I cannot avoid the moral issue and I must answer Lenin's question "What is to be done?" "Truthfulness is the master-key," said Gandhi. "Cling everlastingly to the truth," said Adlai Stevenson. But given the uncertainties and complexities involved in "truth" and "truthfulness," such advice is empty. So what is to be done?

The answer is disarmingly simple: enter the debate. But do so in a way that could encompass the advice both of the deconstructing postmodernists and of Adlai Stevenson, at least if one interprets him in a way that he might have found novel. "Cling everlastingly to the truth" must be construed as an instruction to question every assertion that purports to be "*the* truth." But the procedure is not intended to uncover the "real truth" and separate it from an illusory truth. Rather it is directed toward discovering the consequences of having one or another value-truth (which is always a basic lie) prevail. Sometimes this will be Cicero's question "Cui bono?" (Who benefits? Who has a piece of the action?), and the answer to that might move one to contest the basic lie. But there will be other occasions, as in the case of the wedding performances described earlier, or even of "the presence" lording it over his collusive peasants, when those concerned will decide that they like things well enough the way they are.

Do what you will! When power is at issue, "truth" and "untruth" are your instruments.

References

Anderson, Myrdene
1986   "Cultural Concatenation of Deceit and Secrecy." In *Deception:
       Perspectives on Human and Non-human Deceit*, ed. Robert
       W. Mitchell and Nicholas S. Thompson. Albany: State Uni-
       versity of New York Press: 323–48.
Asad, Talal, ed.
1973   *Anthropology and the Colonial Encounter*. New York: Human-
       ities Press.
Bacon, Francis
1909 [1597]   *Essays of Counsels—Civil and Moral*. Harvard Classics,
       vol 3. Ed. Charles W. Eliot. New York: Collier.
Bailey, F. G.
1957   *Caste and the Economic Frontier*. Manchester: Manchester Uni-
       versity Press.
1959   "Politics in Orissa." Nine essays in the *Economic Weekly* Au-
       gust–November.
1960   *Tribe, Caste, and Nation*. Manchester: Manchester University
       Press.
1963   *Politics and Social Change*. Berkeley: University of California
       Press.
1969   *Stratagems and Spoils*. Oxford: Blackwell.
1977   *Morality and Expediency*. Oxford: Blackwell.
1986   "Unto Everyone That Has Shall Be Given." *Public Administra-
       tion and Development* 6:435–44.
Bateson, Gregory
1972   *Steps to an Ecology of Mind*. New York: Ballantine.
Blaxter, Lorraine
1971   "*Rendre Service* and *Jalousie*." In *Gifts and Poison*, ed. F. G.
       Bailey. Oxford: Blackwell: 119–38.

References

Bok, Sissela
  1979 [1978] *Lying: Moral Choice in Public and Private Life.* New
        York: Random House.
Bondurant, Joan V.
  1965 [1958] *The Conquest of Violence.* Berkeley: University of Cal-
        ifornia Press.
Boorstin, Daniel J.
  1963 [1962] *The Image.* Harmondsworth: Penguin.
Bourdieu, Pierre
  1982 [1972] *Outline of a Theory of Practice.* London: Cambridge
        University Press.
Brown, Richard
  1973 "Anthropology and Colonial Rule: Godfrey Wilson and the
        Rhodes-Livingstone Institute, Northern Rhodesia." In Asad
        1973: 173–97.
  1979 "Passages in the Life of a White Anthropologist: Max Gluckman
        in Northern Rhodesia." *Journal of African History* 20:
        525–41.
Cherry, Colin
  1961 [1957] *On Human Communication.* New York: Wiley.
Cornford, F. M.
  1981 [1941] *The Republic of Plato.* New York: Oxford University
        Press.
Coser, Lewis A.
  1956 *The Functions of Social Conflict.* London: Routledge & Kegan
        Paul.
Dutourd, Jean
  1970 *Pluche, or The Love of Art.* New York: Doubleday.
Epstein, T. Scarlett
  1962 *Economic Development and Social Change in South India.* Man-
        chester: Manchester University Press.
Evans-Pritchard, E. E.
  1937 *Witchcraft, Oracles, and Magic among the Azande.* London:
        Oxford University Press.
  1940 *The Nuer.* Oxford: Clarendon Press.
  1962 "Social Anthropology: Past and Present" [1950]. In *Essays in
        Social Anthropology.* London: Faber & Faber: 13–28.
Fest, Joachim C.
  1975 *Hitler.* New York: Random House.
Fischer, Michael M. J.
  1986 "Ethnicity and the Post-modern Arts of Memory." In *Writing*

Culture: The Poetics and Politics of Ethnography, ed. James Clifford and George E. Marcus. Berkeley: University of California Press: 194–233.

Geertz, Clifford
1966 "Religion as a Cultural System." In *Anthropological Approaches to the Study of Religion*, ed. M. Banton. London: Tavistock: 1–46.
1973 "Thick Description: Toward an Interpretive Theory of Culture." In *The Interpretation of Cultures*. New York: Basic Books: 3–30
1984 "Anti Anti-Relativism." *American Anthropologist* 86:263–78.
1988 *Works and Lives: The Anthropologist as Author*. Stanford: Stanford University Press.

Gellner, Ernest
1985 *Relativism and the Social Sciences*. London: Cambridge University Press.

Gluckman, Max
1964 *Closed Systems and Open Minds*, ed. with Eli Devons. Edinburgh: Oliver & Boyd.

Goffman, Erving
1959 *The Presentation of Self in Everyday Life*. New York: Doubleday Anchor.
1961 *Asylums*. New York: Doubleday Anchor.
1966 *Behavior in Public Places*. New York: Free Press.

Hasek, Jaroslav
1973 *The Good Soldier Svejk*. Trans. Cecil Parrott. London: Heinemann.

Hobbes, Thomas
1946 [1651] *Leviathan*. Oxford: Blackwell.

Hobsbawm E. J.
1959 *Primitive Rebels*. Manchester: Manchester University Press.

Hopkins, Thomas J.
1971 *The Hindu Religious Tradition*. Belmont, Calif.: Wadsworth.

Hume, David
1940 [1738] *A Treatise of Human Nature*. 2 vols. London: Dent.

Hutson, Susan
1973 "Valloire." In *Debate and Compromise*, ed. F. G. Bailey. Oxford: Blackwell: 16–47.

James, Wendy
1973 "The Anthropologist as Reluctant Imperialist." In Asad 1973: 41–69.

133

References

Keesing, Roger M.
  1987 "Anthropology as Interpretive Quest." *Current Anthropology* 28:161–76.
Kidder, Tracy
  1981 *The Soul of a New Machine*. New York: Little, Brown.
Kuhn, Thomas S.
  1970 [1962] *The Structure of Scientific Revolutions*. Chicago: University of Chicago Press.
Lacouture, Jean
  1970 *The Demigods: Charismatic Leadership in the Third World*. New York: Knopf.
Leach, E. R.
  1954 *Political Systems of Highland Burma*. London: Athlone Press.
Lenin, V. I.
  1975 [1920] *"Left-Wing" Communism, an Infantile Disorder*. Peking: Foreign Languages Press.
Lewellen, Ted C.
  1983 *Political Anthropology*. South Hadley: Bergin & Garvey.
Machiavelli, Niccolò
  1950 [1513] *The Prince* and *The Discourses*. New York: Random House.
Marx, Karl
  1981 [1852] *The Eighteenth Brumaire of Louis Bonaparte*. New York: International.
Mauss, Marcel
  1966 [1950] *The Gift*. Trans. Ian Cunnison. London: Cohen & West.
Milano, Euclide
  1925 *Dalla Culla alla Bara*. Borgo san Dalmazzo, Italy: Bertello.
Moraes, Frank
  1973 *Witness to an Era: India, 1920 to the Present Day*. New York: Holt, Rinehart, & Winston.
Nelson, John S., Allan Megill, and Donald N. McCloskey
  1987 *The Rhetoric of Human Sciences: Language and Argument in Scholarship and Public Affairs*. Madison: University of Wisconsin Press.
Oliver, Robert T.
  1971 *Communication and Culture in Ancient India and China*. Syracuse: Syracuse University Press.
Polanyi, Michael
  1958 *Personal Knowledge*. Chicago: University of Chicago Press.
Popper, K. R.
  1980 [1945] *The Open Society and Its Enemies*. 2 vols. London: Routledge and Kegan Paul.

Radcliffe-Brown, A. R.
  1957   A Natural Science of Society. Glencoe, Ill.: Free Press.
Rivers, W. H. R.
  1906   The Todas. London: Macmillan.
Rosaldo, Renato
  1987   "Where Objectivity Lies: The Rhetoric of Anthropology." In
          Nelson, John S., et al., 87–110.
Sangren, P. Steven
  1988   "Rhetoric and the Authority of Ethnography." Current Anthro-
          pology 29:405–35.
Schelling, Thomas C.
  1963   The Strategy of Conflict. New York: Oxford University Press.
Schwartz, Theodore
  1978   "Where Is the Culture?" In The Making of Psychological Anthro-
          pology, ed. Geroge D. Spindler. Berkeley: University of Cal-
          ifornia Press: 417–41.
Simmel, Georg
  1964 [1950]   The Sociology of Georg Simmel. Trans. Kurt H. Wolff.
          New York: Free Press.
Spiro, Melford E.
  1986   "Cultural Relativism and the Future of Anthropology." Cultural
          Anthropology 1:259–86.
Strathern, Marilyn
  1987   "Out of Context: The Persuasive Fictions of Anthropology."
          Current Anthropology 28:251–81.
Tyler, Stephen A.
  1987   The Unspeakable. Madison: University of Wisconsin Press.
Weber, Max
  1948   From Max Weber. Eds. H. H. Gerth and C. Wright Mills.
          London: Routledge & Kegan Paul.
  1958 [1904–5]   The Protestant Ethic and the Spirit of Capitalism.
          Trans. Talcott Parsons. New York: Scribner.
White, James Boyd
  1984   When Words Lose Their Meaning. Chicago: University of Chi-
          cago Press.
Wilson, Peter J.
  1974   "Filcher of Good Names: An Enquiry into Anthropology and
          Gossip." Man 9:93–102.
Wise, David
  1973   The Politics of Lying. New York: Random House.
Worsley, Peter M.
  1956   "The Kinship System of the Tallensi: A Revaluation." Journal of
          the Royal Anthropological Institute 86:37–75.

Index

Action, xii, xv, 98, 104–5, 114, 119–
23; freedom of, 3; and ideas, xiii,
xxi; and satyagraha, 24–26; truth
emerging in, xv
Action theory, 100
Acton, Lord, 75n
Adibasis, 40n, 54n, 77–82
Administrators: and anthropology, 72–
74; the collector in India, 77–82;
compiling dictionaries, 107n; Pontius
Pilate, 3; university, xi, xvii, 66. *See
also* Officials
Africa, 73–74, 91, 118
Altruism, xix, 74, 75, 76n, 84
Ambedkar, Dr. B. R., 24n
Amrita Bazar Patrika, 59
Anderson, Myrdene, xi, 68
Anthropology: and colonial administra-
tion, 72–74; as a comparative disci-
pline, 105–14; styles of, xi-xiv. *See
also* Cultures; Ethnographers; Inter-
pretivism; Postmodernism; Relativ-
ism
Anti-Semitism, 115–16
Armstrong, Sir Robert, 2
Asad, Talal, 73n
Athens, 125
Aubrey, John, 21
Audience, 18, 35–36, 59–62, 71, 108–
9, 122
Austen, Jane, 3

Authorities. *See* Administrators; Government; Officials
Authority, 2, 3, 18, 108; of collector,
79; in peasant society, 85–87; of poetic truth, 21; politicians claiming,
62; public opinion as, 75. *See also*
Power

Bacon, Francis, 3; on lies, 2, 27, 65–
66, 71–72, 126
Baden-Powell, Lord Robert, 71
Baderi, 40–45
Barrie, J. M., 32n
Basic lies: xviii, xx, 35–64, 79, 93; in
Baderi, 40–45; and change, 45, 52,
63–64; contested, 52–62; cost of,
63-64; defined, 35–36; epistemologi-
cal foundation of, 122-26; and hege-
mony, 83–84, 91–92; *Leviathan* as,
83; and ordinary lies, 51–52; Plato's
Republic as, 83; of Raj and peasant,
46–52; testing of, 124–26; in wed-
ding ceremony, 36–39
Bateson, Gregory, 32
Bay of Pigs, ix
Bible, 1, 109n. *See also* Pilate, Pontius;
Vulgate
Birth, Kevin, 110n
Bisipara, xiii, 10, 68; cooperative in,
46–51; untouchables in, 42
Blake, William, 97

Index

Index

140

Index

Library of Congress Cataloging-in-Publication Data

Bailey, F. G. (Frederick George)
   The Prevalence of deceit / F. G. Bailey.
     p. cm.
   Includes bibliographical references and index.
   ISBN 0-8014-2542-5 (alk. paper). —ISBN 0-8014-9773-6 (pbk. alk. paper)
   1. Truthfulness and falsehood I. Title.
BJ1421.B335 1991
177'.3—dc20   90-42148